PPC Made Simple

Pay-Per-Click Strategies for Dominating Google AdWords

Michael H. Fleischner

PPC Made Simple

Copyright © 2010 - 2011

Because of the dynamic nature of the Internet, any web address or links contained in this book may no longer be valid.

10 Digit ISBN: 1451527918
13 Digit EAN: 9781451527919

Dedicated to my loved ones—Jamie, Samantha, and Alex, as well as my father for his inspiration and guidance.

Special thanks to my brother for cover updates and ongoing support.

Thanks to Daniel Murphy II for editing work and always having a positive mental attitude

****

Bonus Videos

As a thank you for purchasing my book, I have recorded special bonus videos for you available at:

www.MyPPCmadesimple.com/secret

****

Earnings/Income Disclaimer

Any and all claims or representations as to income earnings in this book are to be considered exceptional results and not average earnings. Your individual results may vary. There is no guarantee that you will earn money using the techniques and ideas in these materials.

Examples in this book are not to be interpreted as a promise or guarantee of earnings. Earning potential is entirely dependent on the person using our methods, ideas, and techniques, and conditions of the marketplace. We do not purport this as a "get rich scheme." Any claims made of actual earnings or examples of actual results can be verified upon request.

Your level of success in attaining the results claimed in our materials depends on the time you devote to PPC, ideas and techniques applied, knowledge, market conditions, and various skills. Since these factors differ according to individuals, we cannot guarantee your success or income level. Nor are we responsible for any of your actions.

There can be no assurance that any prior successes, or past results, as to income earnings, can be used as an indication of future success or results. Making decisions based on any information presented in this book should be done only with the knowledge that you could experience losses. All products and services mentioned in this book are for educational and informational purposes only.

Google is a registered trademark of Google, Inc. PPC Made Simple is not affiliated with Google Inc. in any way, nor does Google Inc., sponsor or approve any PPC Made Simple Product. Google Inc. expresses no opinion as to the correctness of any of the statements made by PPC Made Simple in the materials herein.

CONTENTS

Preface

PPC Made Simple

Preface

After writing my first book, *SEO Made Simple*, I heard from thousands of individuals through letters, blog comments, tweets, and so on who were so grateful that someone took the time to simplify the most difficult SEO concepts, that I knew the same had to be done for pay-per-click advertising (PPC).

From my perspective, search engine optimization was easy compared to PPC. However, as someone with more than a decade of Internet marketing experience, I have been involved with pay per click almost as long as SEO and have spent a considerable amount of time separating fact from fiction.

I thought about how great it would be if I could somehow extract all of my years of learning through trial and error into a short book that could quickly explain PPC best practices, tips, and what has personally worked for me. After giving it a little thought, I knew that creating a simple step-by-step guide to PPC was to be my definite purpose.

As someone who believes in keeping things simple, I wanted to create a book that I would want to read if I was starting from scratch. I know that I learn best when someone takes me by the hand and says "do this" and "don't do this." In this guide, I'll show you what works, explain why it does, and help you to apply it immediately.

The key to becoming successful at PPC is to learn the concepts applied by today's top webmasters, Internet marketers, and super affiliates. Once you learn what to do, it's time to do it. Apply the concepts on a small scale, measure results, and scale it up. PPC doesn't have to cost you an arm and a leg. I'll show you how to start small and use your profits to reinvest in future online marketing campaigns.

Whether you have years of PPC experience or none at all, *PPC Made Simple* will teach you the techniques being applied by the best and brightest to successfully manage online pay-per-click campaigns. Although I cover some general concepts like PPC basics, most of these pages are filled with valuable insights related to the implementation and management of successful PPC promotions.

You may want to read this guide through from cover to cover and then go back and apply each of the concepts that are being taught one-by-one. *PPC Made Simple* is as much a roadmap to PPC success as it is a practical "how-to" guide.

Regardless of your past experience with PPC marketing, this guide will help you start anew. I hope that you not only read this guide but that you use it to improve the performance of existing campaigns and start new ones that grow your business and put money in your pocket. To be successful with PPC, you really only need two things: a willingness to learn and determination.

I. Introduction

Search engine marketing has become a multibillion-dollar enterprise in just the last few years. More individuals, small, medium, and large companies are spending the majority of their marketing dollars on pay-per-click advertising (PPC) than ever before. Ask any business owner about the importance of performance-based advertising, and the response is usually nothing less than "essential."

What's so special about pay-per-click advertising? Before Google AdWords and the concept of pay-per-click advertising were introduced, most marketers were facing basic problems like developing effective ways to measure the success of their promotional campaigns. John Wannamaker, retailing legend, is often remembered for his famous quote, "Half the money I spend on advertising is wasted—the trouble is I don't know which half." This problem had plagued most marketers and business owners until the Internet was born and performance-based advertising was created.

Google with their AdWords program is often credited as one of the first and certainly the most successful form of performance-based advertising available today. Other search engines like Yahoo! and Bing have followed suit, and PPC is now an integral part of doing business online.

According to a recent Jupiter research study, spending on paid search advertising remains on a growth trajectory and will reach more than $26.8 billion this year. Search marketing remains a top priority for marketers, the study found. Some 79 percent of respondents are spending more managing their paid search programs every year, and the majority of advertisers (67 percent) reported that increasing the use of PPC campaigns is a top strategic initiative going forward.

Pay-Per-Click Advertising Offers a Number of Advantages

The reason why so many people are using Google AdWords and other PPC programs is because it offers a number of advantages over traditional advertising and even most other forms of marketing. The first benefit of PPC is the control it gives marketers in managing their budgets on a daily, weekly, monthly, and annual basis. The old model associated with advertising was to either pay each time an ad was shown or for each insertion into a magazine or newspaper. The problem with this form of advertising is that millions of people could see your ad but never respond. And you never knew how many people saw your ad. Furthermore, tracking purchases coming directly from the ad were next to impossible. This reality made advertising a bit of a gamble and certainly suspect in years where marketing budgets were being reduced.

The second advantage of PPC advertising is that it provides the ability to target specific market segments and manage marketing budgets in real time. Add the fact that PPC is one of the most measurable forms of advertising on the planet and you've found the perfect marketing vehicle for promoting your business.

Today it seems that everyone is using Google AdWords in one form or another. Affiliate marketers, businesses selling products, services, and even local retailers have come to rely on PPC to target segmented audiences and promote their products. These businesses understand the power of targeted marketing and the importance of reaching consumers online.

It's clear that pay-per-click marketing is here to stay. Those who plan to market online need to not only be familiar with PPC, but to use it effectively to reach prospective customers and generate profitable revenue.

Learning about PPC

If you're just starting out with PPC or wondering how to generate profitable online marketing campaigns for your business, then you're reading the right book. A number of years ago I realized how important pay-per-click marketing was to my online business and started down the path of learning everything I could about PPC.

Truthfully, I found PPC marketing to be frustrating and difficult to implement at first. Not only did it take me a long time to set up my campaigns, but most of them were losers. They cost me a lot of money with very little to show for it. After running many unsuccessful campaigns, some of them broke even and one or two turned a profit. I focused on the winners and used what I learned to duplicate my success. But it wasn't until I focused on affiliate marketing that I truly realized the importance of PPC and discovered the techniques that turned my PPC marketing from barely turning a profit into a full-time business.

In affiliate marketing, an affiliate promotes other people's products using pay-per-click advertising and other methods like e-mail marketing, traffic exchanges, and social media. Each time an affiliate sells a product, he or she earns a commission. If this commission is more than the cost of the advertising required to obtain the sale, a profit is made. Those making the most sales and the greatest profit are called super affiliates. These individuals are few and have mastered the art and science of PPC.

For super affiliates, it's all about profitability and scale. They often go very broad in their keyword selection and, with the proper tracking, find which keywords generate the greatest return. There's obviously more to it than finding a few really good keywords. Some examples include landing pages, bonus offers, and tracking, but it all begins with a carefully managed PPC promotion.

After many super affiliates become successful and their campaigns require less time to manage, a number of them turn to educating others about pay-per-click and affiliate marketing. The programs they develop are comprehensive but quite expensive. The techniques they reveal, however, are often worth the price. I've gone through my share of pay-per-click and affiliate marketing programs to find new techniques and methods that can take my online marketing to the next level. I'll be sharing many of the techniques I acquired through these courses in addition to those I've learned through trial and error with my own money-making Web sites, as well as those I've used to help improve the effectiveness of my PPC campaigns.

How to Use This Book

Marketing with PPC can be a bit overwhelming at first and difficult to implement if you're trying it for the first time. I'm very familiar with how difficult and frustrating PPC can be. A number of years ago, I started from where you are without the knowledge or practical experience I needed to be successful at the creation, implementation, management, and tracking of online campaigns.

The purpose of this book is to show you how to set up Google AdWords campaigns to successfully market products and services online. Not only do I cover the basics step-by-step, but I'll also be sharing the nuances that make the difference between a winning campaign and a loser.

In this book, I'm going to reveal all I've learned about PPC marketing with a focus on Google AdWords. The same information and techniques can be applied to other PPC networks like Yahoo!, Bing, etc., because what you are about to learn is universal to performance-based marketing and doing business online.

My advice to you is to first read this book cover to cover. Be sure to highlight, circle, or underline any areas that you find particularly helpful and that you want to return to again and again. That's the beauty of having your own copy. Mark it up, turn down the pages, and make it work for you.

As you read the book, you'll notice references to my secret page at http://MyPPCmadesimple.com/secret. There you will find helpful tools, information, videos, and resources that illustrate topics covered and provide additional guidance. You can visit this page at any time to get more information on a particular topic or post a question. Over time I learned that having a community to support your Internet marketing is truly priceless. Make sure to join the PPC community at the Internet Marketing Forum, which is located at http://MarketingScoop.com/Internetmarketingforum.

After reading the book for the first time, the next step is to put together a plan to launch your first campaign or to begin applying the techniques you've learned to existing promotions that you may have given up on. I recommend that you start with a clean sheet of paper and create an outline. Begin with the outline of this book and follow a thirty-day plan where you apply the PPC techniques in the order they were introduced.

To be successful with PPC, you must be willing to win a few and lose a few. Not every campaign will be a winner. Over time, your success rate improves as you launch more campaigns and learn firsthand what is effective for you and what is not. Start small and scale up—this is some of the best advice I can give. It's much easier to make $100 per month than $1M per month. Equally so, it's much more palatable to lose $50 than it is $500.

The best advice I ever got is to think of PPC as pushing a boulder up a hill—it's really hard until you reach a certain plateau. Once you do, the work is much easier. And once over the crest, it works on autopilot. Set reasonable goals and measure your progress along the way. This builds momentum and can carry you during those periods where you're not seeing an immediate return on your investment. In time, you'll get over that hill and will be earning a significant online income.

Chapter Summary

- **Pay-per-click advertising offers a number of advantages.** The first benefit of PPC is the control it gives marketers in managing their budgets on a daily, weekly, monthly, and annual basis.

- **The second advantage of PPC** is that it provides the ability to target specific market segments and manage marketing budgets thanks to the ability to measure real-time performance.

- **Learning about PPC.** Gain experience through affiliate marketing or implementing your own pay-per-click campaigns. Nothing can replace actual experience.

- **How to use this book.** First read this book cover to cover. Highlight, circle, or underline any areas that you find particularly helpful. As you read the book, you'll notice references to my secret page at http://MyPPCmadesimple.com/secret. There you will find PPC related tools, information, videos, and resources.

II. Pay-Per-Click Basics

What Is PPC? Why PPC?

If you're new to pay-per-click advertising or even an experienced veteran, you may benefit from a quick overview of the principles behind PPC and why it is such an attractive way to market your products, business, or services.

Each day, millions of people are conducting research and looking to buy products or services online. As search engines have evolved, Internet browsers have developed certain behaviors to improve the efficiency of conducting everyday tasks like looking for what movies are playing nearby or reading reviews. As individuals use the Web to find information and make purchases, the Internet has been adapting and becoming more efficient.

There is so much information available on the Internet today that consumers have come to depend on search engines to help them navigate through vast amounts of content independently and effectively. Without using an online tool to sift through the billions of Web pages, attempting to find something commonplace, like a local phone number, could take hours.

Search engines provide a way to efficiently locate what you're looking for online. Today, more advanced search engines monitor user behavior and utilize that data to improve search results. In addition to improving the user's experience, Google and other major search engines have found a way to benefit businesses of all kinds too—giving them access to users at the precise moment they are searching for particular content, products, or services (a.k.a. Google AdWords).

Imagine if you had a way to reach specific individuals online at the moment they were ready to buy a product or service. Not only could you reach them at that particular moment, but you could determine what to pay for that opportunity. Having this ability would provide targeted exposure and at the same time give you the ability to manage your marketing budget. This is what PPC advertising is all about—it shows your message to consumers searching for what you have to offer, defining the time, location, and price you're willing to pay. For instance, you can advertise running shoes to those specifically looking for a new pair of running shoes or flip-flops to people who are planning a vacation.

Google AdWords and other PPC providers work off of a bid/ask system. In essence, it's one of the world's largest auctions. You're bidding to get your ad in front of consumers at precisely the right moment and at the right price. This process of bidding can seem complex (as it is based on a number of factors) but can be summed up as paying for the right to display your online ad. In the section on setting bids, we'll talk about the factors that determine your ad's position and price. Once you learn the rules and some tricks of the trade, the process of leveraging the auction to target the right audience to generate sales becomes quite simple.

In addition to having access to the right audience, having the flexibility to promote a variety of products in this auction is also important. What you're advertising with PPC is up to you, but some products will do better than others based on the consumer's decision-making process, product sales cycle, and so on. One of the greatest benefits of Google AdWords or any pay-per-click advertising is that you're only paying for the action itself, the user clicking on your ad, and not the exposure. In my opinion, paying for performance is the most efficient type of advertising available today.

I like to think about online advertising using the analogy of a shopping mall. Lots of people shop at a mall, and many won't be interested in the merchandise your store has to offer. In traditional advertising, you're paying for everyone who walks past your store. With PPC you're only paying for individuals who walk into your store. The difference may seem subtle but it's significant. Those who enter your store have already told us something about themselves— they're interested. Of course, a very small percentage may enter by mistake, but the vast majority is there to learn more about your products or make a purchase.

The same could be said about commercials or magazine ads. Under this type of advertising, you pay regardless of who sees your advertisement. To make traditional advertising more akin to pay per click, advertisers would have to change their mantra to: "It's free to place and ad— we just charge you each time a user calls the one eight-hundred number you've placed in your advertisement." Would you agree that the lead from the ad is more valuable than the ad itself? Of course you would. Someone who has taken an action that indicates firm interest is much more likely to buy than someone who's only window shopping. *Google AdWords is so attractive because you're only paying for advertising that delivers a tangible outcome.*

Your online marketing dollars couldn't be better spent than with PPC advertising. Why waste your money on a billboard that targets every single commuter all the time when you can spend pennies on the dollar for individuals who are actually interested in what you have to offer? PPC delivers warm prospects to you less expensively than virtually any other marketing method and provides benefits not found with many other form of promotion.

PPC is most effective when you have specific goals in mind, set up your campaigns properly, and focus on testing, measuring, and scaling your results. We'll talk about each of these areas in the pages that follow. Once you understand the value of PPC, you're ready to decide what you want to use your pay-per-click marketing for.

What Do You Want to Use PPC For?

Pay-per-click advertising has many uses. Although the primary purpose is to sell something directly, more and more, advertisers are using PPC to build their lists, generate interest around a given topic, or use it to brand their business. There are a variety of ways to benefit from a well-structured campaign that can meet your online promotional needs.

As a lifelong marketer, I boil it down to action. The reason to spend money on PPC is because you want individuals within a target market to take a deliberate action on your behalf. That action may be to fill out an inquiry form, download a whitepaper, buy a product, sign up for a free trial, or use a particular service. Remember, you are paying each time someone clicks on your ad, so make sure you're getting tangible value from that action to generate revenue today or at some point in the future.

I'm often asked whether or not pay-per-click dollars should be spent trying to drive immediate sales or for some other purpose. From my perspective, I like to try to get interested consumers to convert in one step. However, if they aren't ready to buy, I want them to have multiple options that can produce value for both of us. In essence, there is a **hierarchy of actions** I want users to take after I've paid for them to visit my Web site.

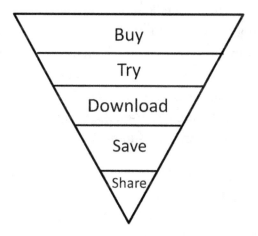

The **PPC Hierarchy of Action**™ illustrates
the steps users can take on a related Web page.

The inverted triangle is set up with the most lucrative action at the top and least desirable at the bottom. Even though you want people to buy immediately after they click on your ad, it may not be possible or even probable that a purchase is made. The next step would be to get users who are not interested in making a purchase to try your product or service. Actions such as download, share, and save are less desirable but better than having a prospect who takes no action at all.

Buy. The reason that most Web site owners purchase traffic through PPC or focus on search engine optimization is to drive prospective buyers to their landing page. The intention is to sell something to those prospects once they arrive. To sell successfully in a single step, you must quickly identify and connect with the needs of your buyers and have them purchase. This is what one would consider an ideal visitor—providing a return on your marketing dollar. Later on, we'll talk about "buying keywords" and how to attract prospects through PPC that are ready and willing to buy. Although more challenging, funneling the right kind of traffic to your Web site increases the likelihood of improving conversions. The first priority associated with your pay-per-click marketing should be, in my opinion, to get prospects to buy.

One might argue that trying to sell a visitor first and foremost may be inappropriate or not ideal based on what is being sold. Some products or services have a long selling cycle, and it may be unrealistic to have someone buy on the first or even subsequent visits. In my thirteen years of Internet marketing experience, it is rare that I've ever seen conversion rates above 1–2 percent. As a result, you can imagine that it takes a significant amount of low-cost traffic to generate profitable conversions. In those situations, it probably makes more sense to move one step down the *PPC Hierarchy of Action.*

Conversion rates are directly proportional to the amount, quality, and cost of traffic associated with your campaign. Additionally, other factors such as landing page quality, offers, and strong calls to action all influence conversion rates. I can't tell you how many times I've worked with companies that need help improving PPC results only to find out that they're driving users to the their home page without a specific call to action or compelling sales copy. Getting prospects to buy in a single step isn't impossible, but it can be difficult.

Marketers have truly expanded their arsenal of conversion tactics including free bonuses, limited time offers, and threats of scarcity. All of these tactics work some of the time but perform differently based on the traffic you attract, your product, and its price. If you're looking to sell visitors on their first visit, be prepared to closely track behavior and measure outcomes. This data can be used to further understand your audience and improve conversion rates.

Try. The old adage "try before you buy" is everywhere. The fact is that consumers like to know what they're getting before they pay for it. With some products, this is easy to do. If you've ever been to the boardwalk by the shore, you've probably tasted a free sample while passing by a candy store or fudge shop. Try it and you're much more likely to buy. Web sites also subscribe to thirty-day, fourteen-day, or seven-day trials to put consumers in the driver's seat, getting them engaged to a particular solution, product, or service.

There have been numerous studies showing that conversion rates are much higher after consumers try a product than if attempting to sell them without a trial. If you are selling a product or service that can provide a trial, consider adding the tactic to your marketing mix. This works extremely well for software or online service providers. Once users are engaged, set up their account, and have begun using the product, it's much easier to purchase the full version as opposed to starting all over again.

A great example of this is a reverse phone lookup. If you've ever tried to look up someone's phone number or address online, you probably found a site that allowed you to enter some information and get a search result. When you view the result, some basic information is provided and access to additional data like "public records access," "credit check," etc., is available for an additional price. This type of offer has a high conversion rate because they've provided something for free and made an offer only after you've shown a strong indication of interest.

Download. When directing prospects to your Web page from PPC advertising, you may consider offering some type of download. This is ideal for sites that are not looking for immediate buyers or able to offer some type of real-time trial. However, the line between "try" and "download" often overlap as some trials do require a download of some kind – others do not. The key take-a-way is that your PPC marketing can be used to generate an action from your Web page. Consumers who aren't ready to buy may be open to a free download that provides tangible value.

Again, remember the purpose of the hierarchy is to get prospective customers to take action. By doing so you are moving them through the purchase decision process and engaging them. This type of commitment is required before a purchase is made. When offering a download, make it simple to sign in, download, and start. Where many sites go wrong is with a long registration process, complicated download, and so on. Think "one click" and apply that methodology to your download. Users should see the benefits of the download and be able to take advantage of your offer quickly.

Once your download is operational, provide users with additional guidance and support. By requiring some type of registration for the download (I recommend name and e-mail only), you can personalize your messages to them over the trial period. Value-added content such as instructional videos and information will reinforce the quality of what you have to offer. Information may include testimonials, features, and benefits. Toward the end of the trial period, develop a sense of urgency by creating scarcity with a limited time offer that includes a bonus and other promotional tactics to yield high conversions.

Keep in mind that not all downloads are in the form of software or free trials. Downloads can also be informational. I've been using free e-book downloads on my sites for years and have built large lists to market products to. As is often said, "the money is in the list," and nothing could be more accurate. Once an individual signs up for a download, you can continue to provide additional value through articles, resources, etc., and begin selling them related products and services.

Save. Often individuals are not willing to exchange information even if the site they are visiting connects with them and offers a compelling download. In these situations, the next best thing is to have the user save your page. This is referred to as *bookmarking*. Sites like Digg, Delicious, and Technorati have become common over the last few years as a place to submit content or keep a virtual list of sites for ongoing reference. On all of your sites, blogs, etc., make it easy for people to bookmark.

Once a bookmark is placed, visitors can return to your site easily. This is important because you never know when they are going to need your product or service. And trust me, bookmarks get used frequently. I can tell from tracking data that some individuals may come back to your site multiple times within thirty days to make a purchase. If you have never placed a bookmark on your Web site or landing pages in the past, I recommend AddThis.com as a good place to start.

Share. Social media is big. In fact, more and more people are using social media every day. Unless you've been hiding, you know that more information is exchanged via social media than through any other means. Think about Twitter, Facebook, MySpace, and other popular social media sites as a conduit to the masses. Clearly having others share your content or offer with friends and family can have a positive influence on conversion rates. Social media is an effective means of promotion because most people buy based on recommendations.

The reason why "share" is at the bottom of the triangle is because the first step is getting visitors to make a purchase. As noted above, they may not be ready to buy or the ideal customer. However, if you've paid for them to visit your site via PPC advertising, it's best to turn that cost into revenue. There's a good chance that they know someone who can benefit from what you have to offer. So make it easy for them to do so.

Put your sharing on steroids. Integrate sharing related icons throughout your Web site and landing pages. If browsers aren't going to buy immediately, try your product, take advantage of a download, or bookmark your site, encourage them to share it with their social network. By making this easy to do, your traffic can multiply significantly. There are plenty of great examples on sites that fully integrate social media options and make it easy to content to large networks of fans, friends, and followers. Don't overlook this simple yet highly effective tactic on landing pages.

Regardless of the action you want paid traffic to take, you must prioritize. Once you've determined the action of greatest priority, design your ads and landing pages around that. I also recommend that you keep the desired action in mind when planning your PPC campaigns. If your main goal is to get individuals to buy from your site, emphasize buying keywords and ads. If the main objective is to get visitors to download a free e-book, focus your keywords and ads on free downloads and the benefits of consuming the offer. This is why beginning with the end in mind is so important for creating effective PPC campaigns.

PPC Definitions

By now you know that pay-per-click marketing is ideal for anyone doing business online or looking to drive traffic to a Web site, blog, or retail establishment. Before I can teach you advanced techniques associated with PPC and making money through online advertising, I first need to cover some basics. If you're already familiar with PPC, then feel free to skip this section but keep in mind that I'll be referring to these concepts again and again throughout this book. Therefore, should you have any doubts about your own knowledge, consider spending a few minutes reviewing the concepts below.

Pay-per-click advertising: Any form of online advertising where advertisers pay each time their ad is clicked by a user.

Users are then directed to a specific web page determined by the advertisers. Keep in mind that pay-per-click advertising is also available on other search engines like Yahoo and Bing. Although Google is the dominant player in PPC marketing, expanding your campaign to other search networks can be very profitable.

Impressions: The number of times searchers see your ad.

Impressions are based on a number of factors. For example, your ad being displayed is influenced by how many times people search for your keywords, how large your budget is, the number of ads competing for the same keywords, and how high your bids are. If you're bidding on terms that are rarely searched, you will not have many ad impressions. Additionally, if you have a low budget, your ad may not show on every search query. If it did, you'd run out of money very quickly. And if your bids are too low, you may appear lower on the search results page or on the second or third page of results, because others are willing to pay more to have their ads shown.

Clicks: The number of times searchers click on your ad.

People click on your ad when they think it matches what they are looking for. Including keywords and a call to action in your ads make it more likely customers will click. If you want more clicks, you need to make your ads enticing to prospects. More clicks mean more traffic and possibly more sales via your Web site. For example, if your customers want free shipping and you offer it, state that offer it in your AdWords ad.

The key to being successful with PPC advertising is to attract the right type of clicks. That is to say that anyone can pay for the highest bid for a generic term. Doing so, they will appear at the top of the page and generate a lot of clicks. However, the number of conversions they receive are going to be poor. Appealing ads that are not relevant to a browser's search result in what I like to refer to as "worthless clicks". This is true for those who think they need to be in the number one position for a given ad. If you create an ad that is unrelated to your offer, then you're going to incur costs with no corresponding revenue. Be smart. Keep your ads targeted to your offer and within ad positions 3–8 to avoid the worthless click syndrome.

Click-through rate (CTR): The percentage of time that people click on your ads in proportion to the number of impressions you receive (CTR=clicks/impressions).

If you received one thousand impressions and twenty clicks, your CTR is 2 percent. CTR can indicate how relevant your customers find your ads and keywords—and Google is ALL about *relevance*. Remember that not everyone who sees your ad is going to click on your ad. Some people will click on competitors' ads or on organic search results and others won't click on anything. Keep in mind that 86 percent of clicks on Google's first page of search results go to organic search and about 14 percent go toward paid search. This means that you will always have more impressions than clicks.

The main focus for most online marketers is increasing the number of clicks they receive on their ad. Based on a higher budget and more click activity, Google rewards the Internet marketer with a lower cost per click. To raise CTR ads need to be more appealing to the target audience. Try including keywords and call-to-action phrases to make ads more relevant to your customers' searches. We'll cover other techniques to improve click-through rates later. For now, just know that you are striving for higher click-through rates on ads. I will show you some specific techniques that can improve your CTR rate and drive down costs.

Though impressions, clicks, and CTR all give you good indications of how well ads are performing, the best way to measure the effectiveness of your online advertising is to calculate your return on investment (ROI).

Return on investment (ROI): The amount of profit generated from your online marketing promotions.

To be successful online, one needs a clear understanding of how much money is being made on each campaign. If you don't think ROI is important, then you probably won't be in business for long. Making money through PPC is literally a numbers game. Know your numbers and focus on profitability.

A positive return on investment can be explained as the amount of money made for each dollar spent. If for example I spend $1 on pay-per-click advertising and make one sale that generates $1.50 in revenue, I've made fifty cents in gross profit. This return on investment is 50 percent—earning fifty cents for each dollar spent. This is helpful to know because you want to focus on campaigns that generate the highest positive return and concentrate on improving break-even campaigns and shutting off the unprofitable ones.

Chapter Summary

- **What is PPC? Why PPC?** Pay-per-click advertising is one of the world's largest auctions. You're bidding to get your ad in front of individuals at precisely the right moment (when they are making a buying decision) via a bidding process. This process can seem complex as it is based on a number of factors but can be summed up as paying for the right to display your online ad.

- **What do you want to use PPC for?** Have a clear understanding of what you'll be using pay-per-click advertising for. Review the *PPC Hierarchy of Action* to determine the specific actions that users, who are attracted to your site through pay-per-click advertising, should take: **buy, try, download, save,** or **share.**

- **PPC Definitions.** Before starting any PPC campaign, familiarize yourself with common names given to different aspects of performance-based marketing, which include the following:

Pay-per-click advertising—Any form of online advertising where advertisers pay each time their ad is clicked by a user.

Impressions—The number of times searchers see your ad.

Clicks—The number of times searchers click on your ad.

Click-through rate (CTR)—The percentage of time that people click on your ads in proportion to the number of impressions you receive (CTR=clicks/impressions).

Return on investment (ROI)—The amount of profit generated from your online marketing campaigns.

III. Setting Up Your First Campaign

Here's where the rubber meets the road. I'm assuming that since you're interested in PPC advertising you already have a product, service, or Web site you wish to promote. If not, don't worry. There are plenty of resources online that can teach you the art of affiliate marketing (selling someone else's product online and earning a commission) and dozens of affiliate networks like ClickBank and Commission Junction for finding products to promote that can earn you commissions and secondary income streams.

PPC advertising works best for products with relatively high profit margins. Because you pay each time someone clicks on your ads, keeping click costs low and profits high is a top priority. When setting up your first campaign, focus on products with high margins. By doing so, you're increasing the likelihood of running a profitable campaign. As your experience with PPC grows, you'll have the knowledge required to effectively manage costs and have higher conversion rates resulting in more profitable campaigns.

Choosing a product to promote should be based on the needs of your business, profit margin, and sales process. Some time ago, many affiliates made the majority of their commissions through what's called direct linking. They would simply promote a tracking link through pay-per-click advertising, driving targeted traffic to a merchant's page. When the traffic converted to a sale, they received a commission. This required no product knowledge and resulted in relatively high profit margins.

Google has cracked down on this practice, limiting the number of competing ads for a given Web site (no two ads with the same display URL can be shown simultaneously). This has created a growing focus on landing pages, review sites, and improved Web site design. To create effective ads, landing pages, and so on, you need a good understanding of your product's features, benefits, and the audience you're trying to reach.

Now I'm going to get you started creating your own pay-per-click campaigns for whatever type of product you wish to promote. Not only will I quickly cover the basics, but I will also provide the tips and strategies I've learned to dramatically improve PPC results.

Step 1: Open up a Google AdWords Account.

Let's start from the beginning. You can join any one of a number of pay-per-click networks, but Google AdWords is the best. Not only is AdWords the largest but from my experience has always generated the greatest returns. I've run PPC ads on Yahoo! and Bing to scale my results (as I'll share with you later), but have never had the same level of success as I've experienced with Google, which is more than twice the size of its closest competitor.

To open an account, go to *adwords.google.com* and click the "Start now" button.

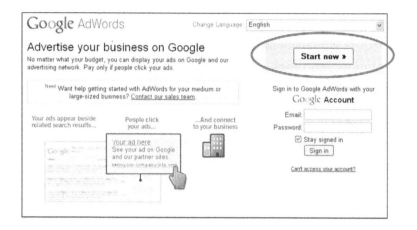

To begin the sign up process, you must select whether or not you already have an e-mail address and password for Google AdSense, Gmail, or iGoogle. Check the appropriate radio button and proceed to the next step. If you do not have an existing account, choose the "I do not use any of these services" and enter e-mail and password. When complete, click the "Create Account" button. You will then be asked to set your time zone and currency and asked to confirm your account by clicking an activation link in the confirmation e-mail that Google sends to the address you provided.

If you need further instructions on signing up, please see the Google AdWords help menu. I don't want to spend too much time on account set up because getting started is easy to do and very basic.

Once you've finished the set up, it's time to put together your first campaign. Whether you are starting your first AdWords campaign or have already tried your hand at Google PPC, I'll be showing you some great techniques for creating and managing your pay-per-click marketing with ease. As someone who uses Google AdWords extensively for my own business, I'm going to share every tip, technique, and trick I use to make Google AdWords both profitable and fun to use.

In just a few short chapters, I'm going to reveal a powerful tool that will eliminate hours of time usually needed to set up winning PPC promotions. However, I'm not going to share this tool with you just yet. It's more important at this time for you understand how to create a winning campaign on your own, without the help of online tools. This fundamental knowledge is critical for helping you understand different aspects of your PPC campaigns and to troubleshoot later when multiple campaigns are running. Once you've learned all of the steps, I'll show you exactly how I upload and manage multiple campaigns, with thousands of keywords, in only a few minutes each day.

After you have logged in to your new account, you will be taken to your AdWords home page. Please note the account I use herein is for illustration purposes only.

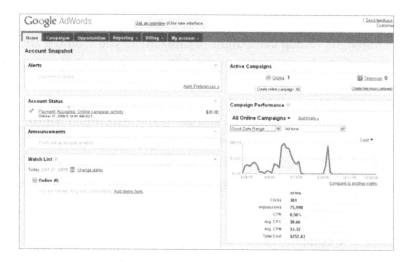

On this page you can view alerts, account status, announcements, and performance criteria such as active campaigns, impressions, clicks, and costs. This page provides a great snapshot of your overall AdWords activity and is the place from which to navigate to any aspect of your Google AdWords campaign.

To quickly orient you, I'll provide an overview of the navigational tabs located at the top of the screenshot above. Please note that you'll be doing most of your work on the "campaigns" tab but need to understand all aspects of your account. To save time, I'll be covering in-depth the "campaigns" only, but please take the time to click through on all the tabs to get familiar with every aspect of Google AdWords.

Setting Up Campaigns

Think of campaigns as being similar to a file folder. I use folders for organizing all of my paperwork associated with any given project. The same holds true for AdWords campaigns. Keep campaigns organized, as you would a file for a particular project, so everything you need to be successful is in one place.

Click on the campaign tab, and there you will find a list of all active, paused, and deleted campaigns along with a snapshot of campaign activity including name, daily budget, clicks, impressions, click-through rate, average cost per click (CPC), total cost, and so on.

If you're completely new to Google AdWords and are wondering what it takes to start your first campaign, click the option that says "Create your first campaign." If you have completed your first campaign and would like to add another one, click the "+New Campaign" button. This button is located under the main graph on the left-hand side of the page. This action takes you to a screen where you can set up campaign details.

Before we start our first campaign, let me walk you through the other tabs within the Google AdWords Campaign section. Please note that for new accounts, these options may not be visible until you have first set up your first campaign. Google will guide you through the initial set up. You can then modify your settings using the following tabs.

The next tab after "Campaigns" is the "Ad groups" tab. Ad Groups are synonymous with themes. Using the folder example, you might put a paper clip on all of the documents related to a single theme. Let's say you were doing research on cars and you named your campaign "Automobile Research." Within the automobile research folder, you may have a number of print outs regarding Toyotas that are held together with a paper clip, a second group of documents relating to Fords held together with another, and a third set paper clipped together regarding Chevys. These bundles are similar to ad groups that contain all of the ads and keywords you have related to any one of the before mentioned bundles.

Said another way, ad groups are the different themes of your campaign. If your campaign is about investing, your themes may include stocks, bonds, money market accounts, and so on. Each of these themes would be considered an ad group. Got the picture? Things will become clearer as we go along and start to create actual campaigns. Again, I will be focusing on more advanced concepts, so this knowledge is required before moving on.

My advanced recommendation is to create a single ad group for each keyword. Okay, stay with me here. Traditionally an ad group consists of multiple keywords and ads, creating a cohesive theme. However, by creating an ad group for each keyword, instead of a large group of them, you improve the relevancy of keywords to ad groups. This means that we are going to create a single ad group for each keyword you are using. I will illustrate this later on but have found this technique to be easy to implement and results in a higher quality score and click-through rate. More on this later…

Settings. Now that we've talked a bit about ad groups, let's focus on the settings for our campaign. This feature is covered when Google walks you through the campaign set up wizard, and later as a separate tab.

After selecting the "Settings" tab, you will find a list of all your campaigns. After selecting one (by clicking on its name), you're taken to the settings for that particular campaign. What are your settings? The settings area provides a good deal of control over where your ads are displayed, how often, and under what budget.

The first place to start is with **location**. I recommend that you run your campaigns in the United States, Canada, United Kingdom, and New Zealand if you are based in the United States. These English-speaking countries provide additional traffic and exposure. Although I recommend the English-speaking countries noted above, when starting out, you may want to limit your reach to the United States and UK only. Make sure that "language" is set to English. If you are not from the United States, simply target the countries where the majority of your customers are from.

Next, focus on the **Networks, devices, and extensions** section. Google wants to know where you want your ads to appear. I have generated results on all devices to varying degrees. "Google Search," which refers to the Google search engine, is a must. Check off the box next to "Google Search" as well as "Search partners." "Search partners" refers to those sites that are promoting Google ads through Google AdSense.

Under content, I would *not* make any selections at this time. The Content Network can be a great way to scale your campaign and generate profits. However, it takes a very different approach involving grouping, which I'll discuss as we start setting up campaigns. Please note that I never run a campaign on the Content Network unless it has already proven to be successful on the search network.

Finally, check off "desktop and laptop computers" next to Devices. This ensures that your ads display to the majority of users. You can also select to display your ads on iPhones and other mobile devices with full Internet browsers, but personally I've had less success with this option. I think those using portable devices are less inclined to buy or convert through sharing their personal information when not using their actual computer. Click "save" and your devices have been selected.

Setting Your Budget

The next section, Bidding and budget, is important to the overall success of your campaign and where you need to give considerable thought. My philosophy on budget is that you shouldn't spend what you don't have. Before starting any campaign, ask yourself, "How much am I willing to spend on testing?" A good rule of thumb is to spend $5 per day per fifty keywords. Said another way, campaign budget can be determined by the size of your keyword list. I like to start with between 50–300 keywords to test a campaign.

Although we haven't talked about keywords in depth, the number of keywords can be used as a guide for sizing your campaign and estimating traffic. Using standard conversion rates of 1–2 percent, ROI and other metrics can be determined as well. My philosophy on spending in general is to start small and scale up once I see success. Truthfully, if I spend $100 on a PPC campaign (assuming that I'm selling a $30 product) and don't see any results, I simply move on. This is why it's so important not to get wedded to any particular PPC campaign.

Don't keep throwing money at the same campaign hoping and praying that it will turn around. I've fallen into this trap, and nothing good ever comes from it. Campaigns don't magically turn around on their own. As we'll discuss later, we want to learn from each campaign, identify the "winners" as soon as possible, and likewise, turn off the unprofitable ones.

Okay. Let's assume that you have a list of keywords for your product or service, and you are going to spend $20 per day in clicks to generate traffic and conversions. For those who are interested in following the math, let's assume a 1 percent conversion rate (one sale for every one hundred clicks). Assuming that clicks are costing me ten cents per click, two hundred clicks will cost me twenty dollars.

If I only sell one product per day (earning $20) and spend $20 in pay-per-click advertising, I break even. However, most products don't have a 100 percent profit margin, so generating revenue that's equal to campaign costs may not be enough. We'll discuss return on investment in greater depth, but for now, simply understand that at a minimum, your advertising spend and revenue generated must be at least equal to one another.

In general, a full week or two of testing is all I need to see if my campaign is profitable. Experience has shown that for every successful promotion I run, five or so are not profitable. Don't be discouraged if your first few pay-per-click campaigns are losers; they usually are. This is one of the most difficult things for individuals working with pay-per-click advertising to grasp. Keep in mind, however, that once you do see a profitable campaign, it can more than make up for all losing campaigns and sustain you for some time.

Under bidding and budget I like to select, "Manual Bidding for Clicks." This allows me to set my limits and closely control costs. Click "Save" and move onto the budget option. Set your daily budget. Again, use the number of keywords as a rule of thumb or determine what you're willing to spend each day to test your campaign. I like to shoot for somewhere in the $10–$30 per day range, depending on the size of the campaign.

For Position preference, delivery method (advanced), choose "Off: Show ads in any position." You will want to change this as you collect more data, but the key thing to keep in mind is that you want top positions at first to see if your ad and landing page will convert. I'd rather know up front if something is going to work or not. After a week of having your campaign up and running, switch this option to deliver your ads in positions 3–6. You can also do this manually using AdWords Editor and other tools. As a final step, select "Standard: Show ads evenly over time" under "Delivery Method" before moving to the next section.

The only thing you need to do in **Advanced settings** is to go under ad delivery and select "Optimize: Show better performing ads more often." Please note that the first time you set up a campaign, the option for "Ad Delivery…" may state that it's "Unavailable" because there is no ad. So keep in mind that first time set up may not offer all Advanced options. After saving your settings in each section, you then move to the "Ads" tab.

If you are setting up a campaign for the first time, now would be a good time to follow the above set up instructions and get started. Basic set up is easy once you navigate it on your own.

Chapter Summary

- For your first campaign, focus on products with a good profit margin. Open a Google AdWords account at adwords.google.com to get started with PPC.

- Get familiar with the Google AdWords navigation tabs by exploring Campaigns, AdGroups, and Settings.

- On the location tab choose English speaking countries if you are located in the U.S.: United States, Canada, United Kingdom, and New Zealand.

- On the Networks, devices, and extensions tab, select all devices for Google Search and Search partners. Do not select the Content Network. Include desktop and laptop computers.

- A good rule of thumb for a PPC budget is $5 per day per fifty keywords. I like to start with between 50–300 keywords to test a campaign.

- For Position preference, delivery method (advanced), choose "Off: Show ads in any position."

- After a week of having your campaign up and running, switch this option to deliver your ads in positions 3–6.

- Advanced setting, go under ad delivery and select "Optimize: Show better performing ads more often."

IV. Keywords

How do you choose the right keywords? This is one of the most important aspects of creating profitable PPC campaigns. Although I once struggled with finding the best methods for choosing keywords, I've learned a number of short cuts for finding high-converting keywords before starting any campaign. Of course you can't truly know which keywords will provide the best return until your ads are up and running, but I can show you how to stay one step ahead of the competition.

Anyone who's been around Internet marketing for a while knows about AdWord keyword tools like the one Google provides. In addition however, tools like Keyword Spy, Microsoft's Commercial Intent Tool, and others have sprung up over the past few years making the task of choosing the right keywords even easier.

Let's begin with the Google AdWords keyword tool available at https://adwords.google.com/select/KeywordToolExternal or by searching "Google AdWords Tool." This tool has been around since the beginning of AdWords and provides real data that can help guide your keyword selection process.

Before I show you how to use the tool, let me explain a little more about keywords. Keywords, which are the search terms individuals type into the Google search box, are what drives an ad to appear next to a set of search results. If someone types in "running shoes" and you've already selected "running shoes" as a keyword phrase, your ad may appear when users type this phrase. I say "may appear" because you would need to be outbidding other online marketers for the keyword and have a decent quality score. The thing to keep in mind is that numerous factors like bid price, relevance, and competition come into play. Even if you've selected the keyword "running shoes" but you're being outbid, your ad may not show. Regardless of what the competition is doing, it's important that you choose keywords that will be relevant to your ad, your Web site or landing page, and ultimately your offer.

Let me use the Google AdWords tool to illustrate how to do some very basic keyword research for free. I'll continue with the running shoes example.

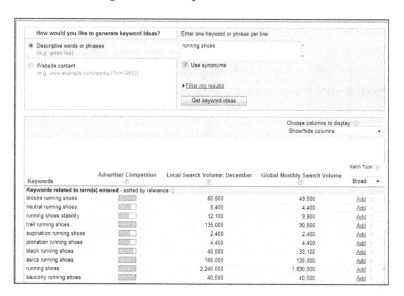

You'll notice that under, "How would you like to generate keyword ideas?" I selected "Descriptive words or phrases." This option is ideal if you are selling a product or service that is easily explained. Just add your keywords or phrases into the available text box and be sure to check "Use synonyms" before entering the CAPTCHA text and clicking the button that says, "Get keyword ideas."

As you can see, a list of related keywords and corresponding search volumes has been generated. The keyword tool returns the exact number of searches conducted for those terms on both a local and global basis for the month. Sort columns appropriately to rank order keywords by search volume. I like to sort by local search volume for the month, giving me a picture of how many times each keyword term was searched in the USA for the last full month. I can also see advertiser competition as more competitive terms will have a higher cost per click.

I usually go through the list and click the "Add" link located to the right of the keyword, building a list that can be exported as a text or CSV file. Select keywords that have a minimum monthly local search volume of 1,500 or more and are related to the products or services you're promoting. Some Internet marketers select all the keywords shown in the results list. However, I begin to eliminate keywords that are too general. For example, I was recently promoting article submission software and selected "article" as a keyword. I decided to include it in my campaign. As a result, I got lots of clicks but no conversions—what a waste! This term was much too general to ever know what someone was thinking about when it came to their search query. Most individuals who clicked on my ad were probably looking to read specific articles on a given topic, not buy article submission software. Knowing how to produce a good keyword list is important for creating a winning Google AdWords campaign.

The second aspect of this tool, which is equally powerful yet rarely used, is the option to search for keywords by URL. I generally plug in the URL of the Web site I'm promoting and the top competitors' Web site(s) to get Google's suggestions on the right keywords. You can do this by selecting the radio button that says, "Website content." After searching by domain, you can add the resulting keywords to your original list that are appropriate for the audience you are trying to reach. Not all keywords are going to be relevant, so be selective.

Both methods of keyword research with the Google AdWords Keyword Suggestion Tool are ideal for use on the Google AdWords Search Network and Content Network. The Search Network is comprised of Google itself as well as other sites that are powered by Google's search algorithm. The Content Network is comprised of other Web sites that display Google Ads around unique information and content. We are going to focus on the Search Network primarily followed by the Content Network, which requires a slightly different strategy of grouping like keywords (up to fifty) to deliver targeted results. I only recommend using the Content Network once you've found a winning combination of keywords, ads, and landing pages.

When thinking about promoting your ads on the Google Search Network, I'm often asked if search volume matters. My answer is that it depends on how many keywords you're working with. When starting out, you want frequently searched keywords because your ad will show more often and produce more clicks. The catch-22 is that the keywords that have higher search volumes may cost more to promote. This is why having a good Google Quality Score is so important and why it's essential to create relevant ads. Truthfully, my highest click-through rates have been among terms that are not as frequently searched but incredibly relevant. An example here might be "cross country running shoes."

Start with the highest trafficked keyword terms you've selected and work your way down. Depending on your search query, you may find that you're right around one hundred keywords—a great place to start! That's essentially all you need to get started. As you become more skilled, it will be common to launch campaigns with larger keyword lists. However, for those just starting out with limited budgets, it's best to test campaigns on a smaller scale and build from there.

Competitor's keyword phrases. For those in search of more advanced keyword generation techniques, let me introduce you to Keyword Spy, SpyFu, Key Compete, and PPC Bully. These online tools help you see what your competitors are doing from a PPC perspective. With all of the before mentioned tools, you can see specific keywords that the competition is bidding on, what ads they're using, and even how long their ads have been running. Ads that have been running for a significant period, usually a couple of months or more are generally profitable for the advertiser.

I've experimented with all of these tools and personally recommend Keyword Spy. I found it to be the easiest to use and most informative. I've also used Key Compete but found the database of competitors to be somewhat limited. As I began promoting new niche markets, Key Compete didn't have much of the competitive information I was looking for when building my keyword list. It is however a decent alternative for those starting out in PPC and promoting more general products. Tools like Keyword Spy and Key Compete are incredibly powerful and can make a huge difference in the quality of your keyword research and the time it takes to generate winning Google AdWords campaigns. But there's a catch. These tools are pretty expensive. Most of them are $100 or more per month but can generate huge lists of profitable keywords.

Super affiliates, those who make a living promoting affiliate products via Google AdWords and other pay-per-click networks, are managing tens of thousands of keywords and campaigns at one time. These individuals are working with large keyword lists to discover the right combination of keywords, ads, and landing pages that lead to high conversion rates. Even so, the number of maximum keywords used by Google is fifty thousand. Essentially, you are limited to ten thousand keywords and two thousand ad groups per campaign. If you are just staring out, you may hit a one hundred ad groups per campaign limit. You can get this changed however. Once your account has been active for at least four months and you have an established track record, you can have your limits increased or removed. You can also call Google directly at 866-246-6453 and ask them to increase your ad group limit from one hundred to two thousand. Be sure to explain that you have a diverse keyword list and want to create several hundred highly targeted ad groups in order to get the best quality score and create the most relevant and targeted ads. If one rep declines, call back and speak to another. Remember that you should never start a campaign with anywhere close to forty thousand keywords. In fact, even if you are more advanced, you should never start with more than one thousand keywords.

Even though Google is my first love when it comes to PPC advertising, other search providers like Microsoft have developed tools that dramatically improve your ad performance on any search network. When I find myself with a really large list of keywords, I use a tool from Microsoft called AdSage to help me cut down my list in a way that helps improve quality score by maintaining a high click-through rate. Note that you will need to sign up for a free account to use this tool. Microsoft's AdSage allows you to enter your keyword list and provides an estimated count of searches performed for each keyword. This allows you to sort from the most trafficked keywords to the least. When launching a new campaign, I only focus on high-traffic keywords. After a few weeks, I'll add others with less traffic because they may convert just as well. Starting with high-traffic keywords first and expanding the list over time generates the click-through rates needed to determine if a campaign will be effective and results in a good quality score.

To reduce your keyword list, including only high-traffic keywords, eliminate ones that according to AdSage haven't had at least one search in the last six months. This seems to be a good method to trim keyword lists. Keep in mind that the Microsoft counts aren't always accurate. That's okay though, as they are directionally correct and we are using the methodology to remove keywords with little or no activity.

Another great tool that Microsoft has developed is the **Online Commercial Intention** tool. This free tool allows you to determine the likelihood of an individual, who uses a particular search phrase, to buy after conducting a search. That's right. This tool can help identify what are called "buying keywords." An obvious example would be typing "running shoes" into the commercial intent tool and receiving a rating of "Commercial Intention .99." The closer the result is to the number 1, the stronger the intent to purchase. Currently, there does not seem to be a bulk submission option from Microsoft for the Commercial Intention tool, but if you want to spend the time, filter your keywords by Commercial Intention to improve click-through rates and conversion percentages. The Commercial Intention tool is available at http://adlab.microsoft.com/Online-Commercial-Intention.

Regardless of what method you use, Google Keyword Tool or spying on your competitor's ad campaigns with a tool like Keyword Spy (yes, it's legal), the goal is to find highly relevant keywords that get an adequate amount of traffic. I usually leave off anything that has fewer than 1,500 searches per month. Once you have your list of keywords completed, you're ready to upload them into Google AdWords. Again, I'll show you an easier way to do this using **Google AdWords Editor**, but first you need to complete the keyword research.

The key to effective keyword research is to start small, generate some activity, and measure the results. Use the Google Keyword Tool to begin your campaign and expand your list using competitive research tools. Filter results using Microsoft's AdSage and Commercial Intention tool. The result is a short list of effective keywords that can work with any pay-per-click campaign.

Keyword Match Types

After you have selected the keywords you want, it's time to upload them into AdWords. You can set each search-targeted keyword to have one of four settings. Because you don't know exactly how users will be entering your keyword into the search box, matching options allow you to define the type of searches that you are interested in. Let me explain what I mean by describing each match type and the symbols used to define them. For this example, I'll be using the same keyword we worked with previously.

Broad match: sneakers
By entering your keyword without punctuation, your ad shows on similar phrases and relevant variations. Essentially, anytime someone types a phrase using the word *sneakers*, your ad will appear. He or she could be typing in "sneakers," "running sneakers," "sneakers for free," or "where can I find red sneakers with a blue stripe." The variety of phrases that users can enter is virtually endless, so use the broad match option very carefully.

Phrase match: "sneakers"
Putting quotes around your keyword allows your ad to show for searches that match the exact phrase. The exact phrase means that your keyword *must* be included in the search query. With phrase match, if someone enters "sneakers" or a longer search phrase including the keyword (ex: "running sneakers"), your ad will display. It doesn't matter how long the search query is. If your phrase appears as you've defined it, your ad shows.

Exact match: [sneakers]
When choosing the exact match option, you eliminate any search term variations. No additional words can appear in the search query before your keyword or after it. When Google says exact they mean it.

Negative match: -sneakers
Even though most Internet marketers overlook this powerful option, negative match helps to filter out the types of search queries you do not want. The most popular example is the word "free." If I am selling sneakers online, I'm not interested in users who search for "free sneakers." Using this option, I could apply this feature to a specific keyword or all keywords in my campaign. Don't be afraid to use negative keywords. In fact, make sure that each of your campaigns has a set of well-defined negative keywords before you begin.

With some options, you'll enjoy more ad impressions, clicks, and conversions. With others, you'll get fewer impressions that are more targeted. I prefer to use phrase, exact and negative match types when setting up my campaigns. This guarantees that the keywords I've selected are in each search query. When using broad match types, you really don't know what someone is looking for. I wouldn't want to pay for someone researching "how to pack sneakers for a business trip" or some other ridiculous search that has nothing to do with my campaign. By applying the appropriate matching options to your keywords, you have the best chance of meeting your ROI goals.

To add your keywords, begin by selecting or creating an Ad Group. Once an ad group has been created, select that ad group by clicking on its name. You will then have an option (the button says "add keywords") available. Enter the keywords you want associated with that ad group using the phrase, exact, and negative match types we covered.

Adding the keywords to Google AdWords the old-fashioned way is simple but takes a bit of time. Google recently added a feature that lets you "add by spreadsheet." I encourage you to check out this feature as it saves a good deal of time and effort. However, if you read my last book on search engine optimization, *SEO Made Simple*, you know that I like people to experience the manual method of entering information at least once before using a tool so they understand the mechanics of what is being accomplished. Once you know how things work, you can use tools to help you complete necessary tasks more quickly. And I'll be showing you how to leverage the best tools for doing this work shortly.

Chapter Summary

- Use the Google Keyword Tool. Make sure to have "use synonyms" box checked. Also, remember to add keywords from "Additional keywords" to the Google Keyword search box to get an even broader list of keywords. Use competitors' URL.

- Pick competitors on Key Compete or any tool that provides smaller keyword lists. I strongly recommend this strategy—be sure to find a competitor with a quality keyword list.

- Use the Google Keyword Tool for your initial list, and then use Key Compete or any keyword tool for lateral, broad keyword ideas to add to your list. You may also plug in new keywords you find in Key Compete into the Google Keyword Tool.

- Use the Google Keyword Tool or AdSage to filter out low-performing keywords.

- Reduce your list of keywords to a manageable size. Start with less than one thousand keywords.

- Choose specific match types such as broad, phrase, exact, negative.

- Display your ads across Google Search Network.

V. Writing Powerful Ads

Before I explain how to load ads into Google AdWords, let's talk about what makes a great ad and how you should structure them. What I consider to be a great ad is one that generates targeted traffic. If all you are focused on is creating an ad that gets a high click-through rate, you may be missing the boat. Your goal should always be to create a relevant ad that generates the right traffic. Yes, you want a high click-through rate but only from people who are interested in your offer.

The word that I keep coming back to here is *relevance*. Google is looking for relevant keywords combined with relevant ads that lead to relevant landing pages. When you create consistency in this manner, you lower costs and improve your results. Ads that are relevant get a higher click-through rate than non-relevant ads. I like to see a CTR of between 3–5 percent. Conversion rates (clicks to sale) are usually around 1 percent or less. Let's get down to it and explore the anatomy of a well-written PPC ad.

I'm often asked, "What's the secret to writing great ads?" My answer is always the same—testing. What you think is a great ad or what I think is a great ad isn't important. It's the actual measurable results that truly matter. The key is to create multiple ads and measure their effectiveness.

Before we break down each aspect of your ad, let's discuss some ad-writing basics. While you want your ads to reflect the theme of your keywords, try adding different elements that highlight the benefits of your product or service. For example, if you're selling running shoes, try one ad that talks about different types of running shoes and another that talks about any discounts or special offers you may be running (pun intended). This type of testing will help you identify which ad theme generates a better return for your advertising campaign.

Headline. Each ad begins with a headline. The headline is the *most* important aspect of your ad. As mentioned earlier, it needs to be relevant to the search term that an individual is using. Believe it or not, I find the headline to be the easiest part of constructing an ad. I realize that my methods may be different from the masses, but it gets results. Your headline should be the same as the keyword phrase you are bidding on. That's right—your HEADLINE should be the same as your KEYWORD PHRASE when possible.

By placing your keyword in the headline, you are dramatically improving the relevance of your ad. The only limitation is that Google AdWords headlines have a maximum limit of twenty-five characters. Keywords that are more than twenty-five characters need to be reduced to fit this limitation. There is a great formula in Excel that can tell you how many characters are in a cell. What I like to do is to place all of my keywords in an Excel spreadsheet and use the **LEN formula**. This formula simply counts the number of characters in a given cell and returns the value. I then sort the LEN formula results from most characters to least. I then modify all those keywords that are over the character limit. This saves a lot of time and effort when managing large keyword lists. Check out my free video at http://MyPPCmadesimple.com/secret to see how I do this using Excel. A final note on headlines: make sure that each word begins with a capital letter. You can use the PROPER command in Excel to automate this process. This is a great shortcut that can also be used for the ad itself.

An example of using a keyword and headline appropriately is as follows. Assume your keyword is "Running Sneakers." You may be tempted to create a headline that says, "Running Sneakers On Sale Now." However, the phrase has too many characters. For my ad title, I would only use "Running Sneakers." You might be asking, why not use "Running Sneakers On Sale," which is less than twenty-five characters, or "Buy Running Sneakers"? Although technically either option would work, we're first and foremost concerned with relevancy. By having the ad title match the keyword phrase being searched on, we are creating a significant amount of relevancy for both Google and the consumer. Users who type the search phrase "Running Sneakers" into the Google search bar are more inclined to click through on the ad with a headline that is an exact match to their search query. So don't overcomplicate things—keep it simple. Use your keyword as the headline of your ad to generate high click-through rates.

Ad copy. The next step is to write two lines of ad copy. Keep in mind that each ad written needs to be compelling, have a strong call to action, and of course, be relevant. I like to repeat the keyword I'm targeting in the ad headline *and* the body of the ad itself. Google highlights the keyword matching a user's search query when it appears in an ad. Having the keyword bolded in two places improves click-through rate by making the ad stand out.

Before you create your copy, take note of this next guideline. You should *always capitalize the first letter of each word* in your ad—except for *an, the, and, but, or, of, from, in, to, with,* or *without,* unless it is first word in your ad. This is referred to as initial caps because you are capitalizing the first letter of each word. Studies have shown that initial caps improve click-through rates and make a difference in overall ad performance.

Always write one complete thought per line. It took me a long time to discover this helpful tip. Ads that are easier to read are more active, and you should be using each line to craft your complete thought or idea. When sentences wrap to the second line, readability decreases and your click-through rates will decline. If your first sentence is longer than the space allotted, revise it. Again, keep things simple—one complete thought per line.

In addition to using initial caps and having each line reflect a complete thought, I always make sure that a *strong call to action* is part of the ad. I place my call to action in the second line of the ad. Calls to action include power words like "buy," "sale," "act now," "limited quantities," "free download," etc. Regardless of what phrase you choose, remember that being relevant is often not enough. Prospects only become buyers when led through the purchase decision process. Entice them to take the first step with a strong call to action.

Now that you know how to write your headline, include your keyword in the body of the ad, use initial caps, have a complete thought on each line, and include a strong call to action in your ad, let me give you some additional tips for getting started with writing winning ads. Remember that Google only provides a space of twenty-five characters for your headline and thirty-five characters for each line of body copy. This makes ad writing challenging but not impossible.

Here are some additional ad-writing strategies to jump-start your ad creation:

1. Open a spreadsheet and then do a search on Google for each of your targeted keywords. Begin with the phrases that receive the most traffic (use the Google Keyword Tool available at https://adwords.google.com/select/KeywordToolExt ernal) and enter each ad that appears in positions 3–8 on the search results. You want to do this for your top-searched terms because these ads are already seeing the most traffic and costing Internet marketers a pretty penny. Ideally you want the ads that have been around for some time. This likely means that the ads are producing a positive return for the marketer. Record the ads in the spreadsheet including headline, body copy, and display URL, and today's date. Every few days over a two-week period, duplicate the search. If the same ads appear over this timeframe, it's likely they are winning ads. Use these ads, with slight variation, for your campaign. You don't want to duplicate the ads

exactly, but can certainly use them as a starting point. Explore using tools like PPC Bully or Keyword Elite to duplicate winning ads.

2. Write your first line of ad copy directly about a keyword. Make the second line an offer or call to action. An example of this would be the following ad for running sneakers:

Running Sneakers
New Running Sneakers In Stock.
Special Pricing Available. Buy Now!
www.DiscountSneakers.com

For higher click-through rates, use numbers in your ad. Studies have shown that by using numbers or symbols, you can improve ad click-through rates and even conversions. Here's an example:

Running Sneakers
More Than 300+ Sneakers In Stock.
Special Pricing Available. Buy Now!
www.DiscountSneakers.com

These ads meet all of our criteria for a well-written AdWords ad. It includes the keyword "running sneakers" in the headline, uses it again in the body of the ad, focuses on the keyword (ad line #1), uses a complete thought on each line, initial caps, and has a call to action.

3. Capitalize the first letters of each word in your Display URL (ex: DiscountSneakers.com). If your URL was simply "discountsneakers.com" you can see that it doesn't have quite the same impact as using initial caps.

4. Test multiple ads. Whenever I run a campaign, I test more than one ad. It's always a good idea to try a couple of different approaches. Try to write one ad with a strong benefits statement or one that asks a question. Each market responds differently to ad copy, so testing is paramount. Many times I've assumed that one ad would outperform the other only to find out I was wrong. Let Google be your guide and the stats rule the day.

5. Test different elements. If you want to know specifically what in your ad works well, test only one element at a time. For example, after finding a "winning" ad, change only the headline and keep everything else the same. After you determine which headline works best, you can keep the headline the same while you test the rest of the ad text.

6. Test destination URLs. You can also test out which landing pages work the best for your ads. To do this, run two or more ads with the exact same text but have a different destination URL for each one. For example, if you feature products in your ad, one test could be done by having one destination URL

go to a page that highlights product information and another that goes to a page with product reviews.

Here's the good news. You don't need to create dozens of ads. I launch the majority of PPC campaigns with only two ads. That's right. Even if I'm promoting thousands of keywords, I only use a maximum of two ads, each with a unique headline. As the campaign gets traffic and conversions, I determine which ad is outperforming the other and replace the bottom performing ad with new ad copy. This allows me to continually increase the effectiveness of my ads, improving click-through rates and lowering costs.

Entering ads into Google. To enter ads into Google AdWords, simply fill in the boxes provided on the ad entry screen. Google provides five text boxes to be completed. One for the title, two boxes (one for each line of your description), a line for your display URL, and a final line for the actual URL where users will be directed once they click on your ad. The redirect URL is not visible in your ad, so many advertisers choose to use a tracking URL that will provide analytics that can improve ad effectiveness.

The challenge you face is that every ad group and keyword requires an ad to be entered—even if you're using the same ad. This can be a time-consuming process if running campaigns with hundreds or even thousands of keywords. Google has simplified the process somewhat by repopulating your ad as the starting point for each entry. Even so, I don't like doing this manually for large campaigns. Fortunately, there are tools that can help to automate this process, increasing the speed and accuracy of uploading ads.

Now that you know how to write ads and enter them into Google AdWords, one thing to remember is that higher click-through rates and quality scores mean lower costs. By structuring ads properly, you'll find that the appropriate people are searching and clicking through on your ad. When you have a high click-through rate (anything above 2 percent), Google rewards you with higher placements and lower click costs. Focus on ad writing using the guidelines above to improve traffic and the quality of visitors you're attracting to your Web site or landing page.

One final note on ads. It's important to always be reviewing and monitoring ad performance. To evaluate the success of your ads, compare their performance data. Start by looking at click-through rates. If you are using conversion tracking, look at conversion rate. Some ads will generate more clicks but not convert as well. You want to make sure that you have enough data (impressions and clicks) before making any assumptions or choosing a winning ad. I like to use online tools like those found at http://www.websharedesign.com/tools/ppc-ad-split-testing-tool/ for PPC Ad split testing. After you've determined which ads are performing well, delete your least successful ad and test a new one using the same theme (discounts, benefits, etc.).

Chapter Summary

- Great ads are relevant. This includes relevant keywords combined with relevant ads.

- Click-through rates should be between 3–5 percent. To improve click-through rates and conversions, test multiple ads.

- The headline of your ad should be the same as your keyword phrase when possible.

- Headlines have a character limit of 25 characters. Use the LEN formula to count number of characters.

- Use the PROPER formula to create initial caps.

- Write two lines of ad copy, including your keyword and be sure to use initial caps.

- Make ad copy actionable and relevant to your keywords.

- Follow the eight ad writing strategies noted within this chapter.

- Use only two ads and each with a unique headline.

- Remember that higher click-through rates and quality scores mean lower costs. Properly structured ads generate higher click-through rates.

VI. Google AdWords Editor

I was debating how I should start this section. The first heading I came up with was "The Most Important PPC Tool You Can Ever Use." However, I realized that the Google Keyword Tool we talked about earlier for finding keywords is just as important as this one. Nonetheless, the Google AdWords Editor saves you time, improves results, and makes PPC more enjoyable.

What is Google AdWords Editor? This free tool from Google was developed for online marketers to compile AdWords campaigns offline and upload them to Google AdWords when they are ready to launch. Not only does the ability to work offline help in situations where you may not have an Internet connection, but it also ensures that you're not actively running campaigns until they're truly ready to go. I like the AdWords Editor most of all because when I'm working with campaigns that have literally thousands of keywords, I could never process them manually through the Google AdWords online interface—it would take forever. I've alluded to this tool throughout the book because it really is the key to effectively managing all of your PPC campaigns.

To start, visit http://www.google.com/intl/en/adwordseditor/index.html through your favorite Web browser or simply *Google* "Google AdWords Editor." The page looks like this:

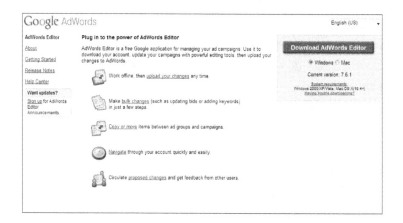

Click the download AdWords Editor button to get started. The first time I downloaded this tool, I was having trouble finding its location on my hard drive. Hopefully, by the time this book goes to print, Google will have integrated a feature to create a desktop icon for you automatically. However, you will find access to the editor using your Start Menu. If not, after the installation, search for the location of the download file on your hard drive and drag the AdWords Editor icon to your desktop. It looks something like this:

Double-click the icon to open the tool and you'll find a simple interface that can be used to build and upload your Google pay-per-click campaigns. When you open Google AdWords Editor, it needs to be associated with your Google AdWords account. As a first step, you can login using your Google AdWords account information or simply click on "file," "open account," and click "Add account."

If you already have a Google AdWords account that includes some existing PPC campaigns, AdWords Editor can synch and download them via the "Get Recent Changes" option. For purposes of this lesson, I'll assume that you have downloaded the AdWords Editor, associated it with your online account, and are ready to begin working on setting up a new campaign. Don't hesitate to use Google's help section. Unlike most online help sections and FAQs, the information is very helpful, and you can often get the answers you need about the Editor without getting frustrated. You can find the help section by visiting: http://www.google.com/support/adwordseditor/?hl=en or by searching Google for "help with Google AdWords Editor."

When inside the Editor, you'll notice tabs across the top of the main window. These tabs include "Keywords," "Placements," "Negatives," "Ads," "Ad Groups," and "Campaigns." Each tab represents an aspect of your AdWords account that we've already discussed. Here's where the magic begins. We are not going to enter each ad group, ad, and keyword manually. The only section we type directly into the editor is for campaign set up. Setting up your campaign parameters takes less than a minute and can be done using the basic interface. All other information will be entered by using a spreadsheet and then uploaded directly to the Editor. Once we check the campaign details for accuracy, we can select "Post Changes" and BAM! You're all done.

Setting up your spreadsheets. In order for AdWords Editor to work effectively you must create spreadsheets that contain the right information and are set up properly. I will show you how to do so here.

The best method for organizing your spreadsheets is to set up a workbook that includes multiple spreadsheet tabs. If you have never worked with spreadsheet before, I recommend you pick up a book or view a tutorial on Microsoft's Web site. Microsoft Excel, which is the most popular spreadsheet software, is available on most computers. Alternatively you can use OpenOffice.org available at http://www.Openoffice.org which provides free spreadsheet functionality.

When setting up my Excel workbook, I make sure to create four separate tabs. The first tab is a general tab that I use to paste my keyword list into. The second tab is labeled "Ad groups." This is where I lay out all of my ad groups and corresponding information such as campaign name, ad group name, and maximum cost per click. The third tab is labeled "Ads" and will not only include two versions of an ad for each ad group, but additional information related to the campaign. And finally, the fourth tab is labeled "Keywords." This includes keyword information including match type (exact, phrase, broad).

Let's start with the Keywords tab on our spreadsheet. I like to start with keywords because we've done the research at this point, and the keywords are "burning a hole in our pockets." Begin by typing the following into row one of your spreadsheet in columns 1–4:

Campaign   Ad group   Keywords   Match Type

These headings are necessary for uploading your keywords to AdWords Editor and helping define specifics related to each word. Create a campaign name that makes sense for your promotion. **Important**: Always make sure to use your campaign name consistently across all tabs (campaigns, ad groups, ads) in your spreadsheet. Any misspellings or typos and you'll receive multiple errors. Unfortunately, I've had to learn this the hard way—many errors that occur within the Editor are the result of errors in campaign name. When setting up your spreadsheet, copy and paste content as often as possible to minimize errors.

Under each heading, enter your keyword information. For example, under the "Campaign Name" heading, you will call this campaign "Sneakers." Type *sneakers* in the first cell and copy it down.

Skip the ad group column for the moment and paste your keyword list under the keyword column. The reason I do this before adding the ad groups is because I copy and paste the keywords into the ad group column and then use the PROPER function in Excel to capitalize the first letter of each name. You do not have to do this formatting step, but I'm a bit anal when it comes to setting up my campaigns. Additionally, it allows me to quickly distinguish an ad group title from a keyword. If using the PROPER function, copy and paste your data as "values." This converts the contents of the cell as text, making it easy to copy and paste later.

Although I'm not going to give you a tutorial on how to use functions within Excel, you can be successful by finding an adjacent cell to the one you are trying to apply a formula to and using your "+=" key. To use the PROPER function, type =PROPER(A2) where "A2" is the adjacent cell, and hit return. Your modified content will appear.

After completing the above steps, if you are following our example, you should have about one hundred rows of data all beginning with the same campaign name, followed by ad group, and keyword. The next step is to add match types. Begin by typing in "Phrase" under the column title and copy it down to the bottom. Now we are going to set up "Exact" match. Copy all of your rows. If you have your headings in row 1, copy rows 2 through 101 and paste them starting in cell 102. Yes, we are essentially copying all of the data on the spreadsheet and pasting it below what we already have.

The next step is to go to the column that says "Match Type" and replace "Phrase" with "Exact" for all rows 102 and down. This gives us two sets of data, one with the phrase match option and one with the exact phrase option. I've done this on a smaller scale so you can see what your spreadsheet should look like. As a final step, name your first tab "keywords."

	A	B	C	D
1	Campaign	Adgroup	Keywords	Match Type
2	Sneakers	Basketball Sneakers	basketball sneakers	Phrase
3	Sneakers	Cheap Sneakers	cheap sneakers	Phrase
4	Sneakers	Discount Sneakers	discount sneakers	Phrase
5	Sneakers	Men Sneakers	men sneakers	Phrase
6	Sneakers	Mens Sneakers	men's sneakers	Phrase
7	Sneakers	Mens Sneakers	mens sneakers	Phrase
8	Sneakers	Retro Sneakers	retro sneakers	Phrase
9	Sneakers	Shoes Sneakers	shoes sneakers	Phrase
10	Sneakers	Sneaker	sneaker	Phrase
11	Sneakers	Sneakers	sneakers	Phrase
12	Sneakers	Sneakers Online	sneakers online	Phrase
13	Sneakers	Vans Sneakers	vans sneakers	Phrase
14	Sneakers	Women'S Sneakers	women's sneakers	Phrase
15	Sneakers	Buy Sneakers	buy sneakers	Phrase
16	Sneakers	Jordan Sneakers	jordan sneakers	Phrase
17	Sneakers	Ladies Sneakers	ladies sneakers	Phrase
18	Sneakers	Basketball Sneakers	basketball sneakers	Exact
19	Sneakers	Cheap Sneakers	cheap sneakers	Exact
20	Sneakers	Discount Sneakers	discount sneakers	Exact
21	Sneakers	Men Sneakers	men sneakers	Exact
22	Sneakers	Mens Sneakers	men's sneakers	Exact
23	Sneakers	Mens Sneakers	mens sneakers	Exact
24	Sneakers	Retro Sneakers	retro sneakers	Exact
25	Sneakers	Shoes Sneakers	shoes sneakers	Exact

After setting up your keywords spreadsheet, the next step is to create a new tab for your Ad Groups. Just as its label suggests, you are now going to set up your ad groups. The headings for this spreadsheet should be:

Campaign   Ad group   Max CPC

Setting up a new tab to record your ad groups is easy to do, especially because we already used the PROPER function in Excel to create ad groups for each of our keywords.

Begin by selecting the unique data (first one hundred rows) under the "Campaign" heading and "Ad groups" column. Paste this data on a new spreadsheet beginning with row 2. Now type in your headings: "Campaign," "Ad group," and "Max CPC" using the first row.

Add your "Max CPC," which stands for cost-per-click in column C. My personal preference is to start with a number between $0.50 and $1.00. The reason I set my maximum bid within this range is because I want to determine if these ad groups and corresponding keywords are going to generate clicks.

	A	B	C	D
1	Campaign	Adgroup	Max CPC	
2	Sneakers	Basketball Sneakers	0.70	
3	Sneakers	Cheap Sneakers	0.70	
4	Sneakers	Discount Sneakers	0.70	
5	Sneakers	Men Sneakers	0.70	
6	Sneakers	Mens Sneakers	0.70	
7	Sneakers	Mens Sneakers	0.70	
8	Sneakers	Retro Sneakers	0.70	
9	Sneakers	Shoes Sneakers	0.70	
10	Sneakers	Sneaker	0.70	
11	Sneakers	Sneakers	0.70	
12	Sneakers	Sneakers Online	0.70	
13	Sneakers	Vans Sneakers	0.70	
14	Sneakers	Women'S Sneakers	0.70	
15	Sneakers	Buy Sneakers	0.70	
16	Sneakers	Jordan Sneakers	0.70	
17	Sneakers	Ladies Sneakers	0.70	
18				
19				

See how to do this on video at
http://MyPPCMadeSimple.com/secret

I essentially start high and then reduce the bids after the campaign is up and running for a little while to position my ads in the third through eighth positions. My testing has shown that ads in these positions generally outperform those in positions one and two. Individuals who are paying the highest bids and placed in the first and second position generally pay more per click and see fewer conversions. A good friend of mine used to click on competitors' ads (in positions one and two) and call it the stupid tax. These positions get a lot of lookers who are usually not all that serious about buying.

The final tab we are going to create is the "Ads" tab. Let's begin with our category headings, which include:

Campaign Ad group Headline Description1 Description2 DisplayURL DestinationURL

In a similar manner to how you created the column headings on the last tab, do the same using each of these headings. Once you've labeled each column, go back to the keywords tab and copy and paste the first set of keywords including the "Campaign," "Ad group," and "Keywords" columns. Paste under "Campaign," "Ad group," and "Headline." Remember that we want our keywords to be in our headline. This improves relevancy and click-through rates, and lowers costs.

The only modification we need to make is to create initial caps for the keywords that have now become our headlines. You may have done this on the keyword tab so no further action may be required. However, if you did not create initial caps, do so now using the PROPER function within Excel, which begins with a plus sign: +PROPER(A2). Apply this formula to all of the cells in the Headline column. When finished, select all of the cells in that column and click "copy," "paste values." This removes the formula and allows us to manipulate the content. The next step will be to determine how many characters are in each cell, as Google only allows headlines to be twenty-five characters in length. Any headlines longer than twenty-five characters need to be modified.

Get a count of characters. To find out how many characters are present in each cell, we use the "LEN" formula in Excel. Not a lot of people know this function exists, and chances are you would never need to use it unless you were a PPC marketer. It saves a lot of time, especially when working with hundreds or even thousands of keywords. Place your cursor in the first cell to the right of your first headline and use the LEN function: +LEN(C3). C3 will be the cell reference you are trying to count. After hitting Enter, drag that formula, or copy and apply, to all the phrases you have in the headline column.

	A	B	C	D
1				
2	Campaign	Adgroup	Headline	
3	Sneakers	Sneaker	Sneaker	+LEN(C3)
4	Sneakers	Sneakers	Sneakers	
5	Sneakers	Men Sneakers	Men Sneakers	
6	Sneakers	Buy Sneakers	Buy Sneakers	
7	Sneakers	Mens Sneakers	Mens Sneakers	
8	Sneakers	Vans Sneakers	Vans Sneakers	
9	Sneakers	Cheap Sneakers	Cheap Sneakers	
10	Sneakers	Mens Sneakers	Mens Sneakers	
11	Sneakers	Retro Sneakers	Retro Sneakers	
12	Sneakers	Shoes Sneakers	Shoes Sneakers	
13	Sneakers	Sneakers Online	Sneakers Online	
14	Sneakers	Jordan Sneakers	Jordan Sneakers	
15	Sneakers	Ladies Sneakers	Ladies Sneakers	
16	Sneakers	Women'S Sneakers	Women'S Sneakers	
17	Sneakers	Discount Sneakers	Discount Sneakers	
18	Sneakers	Basketball Sneakers	Basketball Sneakers	
19				

Once complete, each row includes a number that tells you how many characters are in the headline. Your next task is to sort all of the data by your last column. To do so, select all of the data underneath your headings across all rows and columns. From the Excel menu, select Data, Sort, and Custom Sort so that headlines with the biggest count are at the top of your spreadsheet.

Every headline that is more than twenty-five characters will need to be shortened. If your list is small enough, I recommend that you manipulate each headline by hand, rewriting the headline appropriately. If, on the other hand, your list is longer, consider grouping like headlines and writing a single headline to be applied to each group. For long lists of keywords, I sometimes replace all headlines over twenty-five characters with a single headline that is focused on the niche. It all comes down to the amount of time you want to spend getting this right. Again, if you need any help here, go online to my special page or visit the forum mentioned at the beginning of this book.

Now that we've taken care of our campaign name, ad group, and headline, it's time to focus on creating ads. As I mentioned earlier, it's best to test multiple ads. We can do this by creating two ads to promote in conjunction with each keyword or ad group. In the first cell under your Description 1 column, write a compelling statement that is likely to include your keyword—in this case, "sneakers." I realize that using this method doesn't allow you to always include a keyword in the body text, but it does work most of the time. For example: "Running Sneakers In Stock Now." Make sure to use initial caps. Proceed to the Description 2 field and enter the second line of text. Each line should be a complete thought and have a call to action. Wrapping ideas past the first line rarely produces a positive result.

Make sure the ad really sells the benefits of what you are offering and uses at least one complete thought per line. Remember that what you sell needs to be a solution to a problem. What does it sell? What is the solution? How does your life change by using this product? What will happen to your life if you don't get this product? Focus on the biggest benefit and use action-oriented closings:

- Begin your search now
- Free Download
- Start Now!
- Start Here!
- Act Quickly
- Download Now
- Get It Now
- Sign Up Here
- Sign Up Now

For example, one line may look like this: "Special Discounts. Act Quickly!" Remember that ad description lines can be no more than thirty-five characters. Apply the LEN formula or count the number of characters in your description, including spaces. If more than thirty-five characters, your ad lines will need to be shortened. Once completed, apply both descriptions to all of your rows. You can do this in much the same way we created match types. Copy and paste all of your lines and apply your first set of description lines to your first instance of one hundred keywords and your second set of description lines to the second set of one hundred keywords.

Writing ads can be more art than science, but don't let that discourage you. I like to boil down ad writing to the following: using your keyword in the ad if possible, creating a compelling message, using a strong call to action, and including actual numbers in your ad.

Highlighting a special offer or unique selling point can significantly improve your click-through rates.

After creating your description lines, you need to place a display URL in the Display URL cell. Don't waste any space by placing "http:" in your Web address. Rather, use initial caps and begin with "www" or nothing at all. The display URL should be related to the actual URL. Again, this goes back to quality score and relevance. The more alike your display URL and destination URL are, the better.

C	D	E	F
	Description 1	Description 2	Display URL
	Running Sneakers In Stock Now	Special Discounts. Act Quickly!	www.DiscountSneakers.com
	Running Sneakers In Stock Now	Special Discounts. Act Quickly!	www.DiscountSneakers.com
ikers	Running Sneakers In Stock Now	Special Discounts. Act Quickly!	www.DiscountSneakers.com
kers	Running Sneakers In Stock Now	Special Discounts. Act Quickly!	www.DiscountSneakers.com
iakers	Running Sneakers In Stock Now	Special Discounts. Act Quickly!	www.DiscountSneakers.com
akers	Running Sneakers In Stock Now	Special Discounts. Act Quickly!	www.DiscountSneakers.com
eakers	Running Sneakers In Stock Now	Special Discounts. Act Quickly!	www.DiscountSneakers.com
iakers	Running Sneakers In Stock Now	Special Discounts. Act Quickly!	www.DiscountSneakers.com
akers	Running Sneakers In Stock Now	Special Discounts. Act Quickly!	www.DiscountSneakers.com
eakers	Running Sneakers In Stock Now	Special Discounts. Act Quickly!	www.DiscountSneakers.com
Online	Running Sneakers In Stock Now	Special Discounts. Act Quickly!	www.DiscountSneakers.com
eakers	Running Sneakers In Stock Now	Special Discounts. Act Quickly!	www.DiscountSneakers.com
eakers	Running Sneakers In Stock Now	Special Discounts. Act Quickly!	www.DiscountSneakers.com
Sneakers	Running Sneakers In Stock Now	Special Discounts. Act Quickly!	www.DiscountSneakers.com
Sneakers	Running Sneakers In Stock Now	Special Discounts. Act Quickly!	www.DiscountSneakers.com
l Sneakers	Running Sneakers In Stock Now	Special Discounts. Act Quickly!	www.DiscountSneakers.com

The final step to complete our data fill is to add the destination URL. This is the Web address that users are taken to after clicking on your link. If you are using your own tracking software, your URL may be unique for each row, tracking each ad group (and corresponding keyword) that converts for you. If you are using Google Conversion Tracking, no special URL is needed other than the one you want to direct your visitors to. Google Conversion Tracking records all of the necessary information to determine where your sales are coming from. If you're not familiar with Google Conversion Tracking, don't despair. I'll cover this and other tracking tools in our chapter on analytics.

If your destination URL is the same as your display URL, retype the URL using "http://" so it is actionable. Just copying your display URL and pasting it into the destination URL column doesn't work. In our example, the destination URL is http://www.discountsneakers.com. The use of initial caps isn't necessary because users never see the destination URL. After completing your spreadsheet, save it to your computer so you can proceed to the next step.

Uploading Your Data

Your AdWords campaign is now ready for upload using Google AdWords Editor. As a result of taking the time necessary to properly format your spreadsheets, uploading your campaigns only takes a few short minutes to get up and running.

To begin, open AdWords Editor and click on the "Campaigns" tab. Your screen should look like this:

Click the button on the left of the main screen that says "+Add Campaign." Select the drop down option "+Add CPC Campaign."

Take the following steps:

1. Name your campaign. Use the campaign name you selected when creating your spreadsheet.
2. Set the campaign to active.
3. Under "Search Network" choose "Google and Search Network." By doing so, your ads will appear on Google itself and anywhere the Google search is used.
4. Set your daily budget based on the number of keywords you have: $5 for every fifty keywords or simply enter a number you're comfortable with ($10–$35).
5. Under Content Network choose "None." We need to use a different strategy for the content network. For now, let's stick with only the search network.
6. Enter today's date in the "Date" field. Leave end date blank.
7. Select "English" as your primary language.
8. For location, choose United States, Canada, United Kingdom, and New Zealand. Choose multiple locations by holding down the control button on your keyboard (Ctrl).

NOTE: As an alternative, you can go right to the keywords tab to upload your spreadsheet. When done, go to the "Campaigns" tab and manually change the budget, location, targeting, etc.

Your first tab has been completed. Now that you've set up the parameters of your first campaign, it's time to select the ad groups tab within AdWords Editor. We will now start using your spreadsheet to upload data.

Begin by selecting the button that says "+Add/Update Multiple Ad Groups." This option permits us to copy and paste our spreadsheet data. Complete all the necessary options before copying and pasting your ad group information from the spreadsheet. Depending on the version of AdWords Editor you are using, your options may look slightly different, but the principles are still the same. Select your campaign name using the drop down menu. If this is your first campaign, the name you just entered on the Campaign tab should be visible. Next, skip down to the large text box below and copy everything from the Ad Groups section of your spreadsheet, column headings and all remaining fields (If pasting with column headers, select the checkbox at the top that says "My ad group information below includes a column for campaign names").

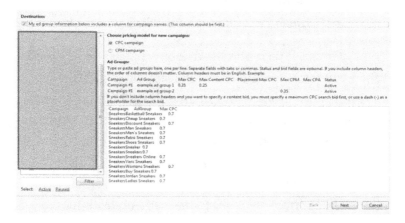

Click the "Next" button at the bottom of the window and then "Finish." At this point, we've successfully loaded our Ad Groups and will move on to Ads. Don't panic when you see the yellow or red caution circle next to your Ad Groups. This is simply indicating that you're missing related keywords and ads for the ad groups you just set up. These warning messages go away as we add the required information.

Click on the "Ads" tab. Similar to the first process, we are going to complete the necessary information on the Ads tab including campaign name. Start by clicking the button that says "Make multiple changes" under the default "Text" tab and select "Add/Update Multiple Text Ads."

When choosing your destination option, choose "My text ad information below includes columns for campaign and ad group names." Under Pricing Model, choose CPC and place your cursor in the Text Ads box. Go to your spreadsheet Ad tab and copy and paste all of the contents (including all columns and rows with content) into the AdWords Editor box where you placed your cursor. Click "next" and "finish" to complete this tab.

The last area we haven't talked about is negative keywords. When you want Google to exclude certain negative keywords (ex: "free") from a particular Ad Group or your campaign, you can enter those through AdWords Editor as well. This ensures that inappropriate search terms do not trigger your ads. When using PPC to market affiliate products, I usually identify negative keyword or keyword phrases like: "free" and "discount." It's not essential to include negative keywords, but some online marketers enter them for every campaign.

Note: From time to time, you may have an error with your upload of campaigns through the AdWords Editor tool—indicated by a red or yellow dot. In these situations, it's best to review the error and make the appropriate changes. If I only have one or two errors, it's generally caused by a duplicate keyword, typo, or missing ad group. Depending on the size of my keyword list, I may choose to delete the error or spend some time understanding how to fix the incorrect code.

Once your ads are entered into the Editor, you're ready to upload them to your live AdWords account. To do so, follow these steps:

1. Click on "Post Changes," which is a button located on the top of your Google AdWords Editor control panel.
2. Select the second radio button that displays your campaign name. In this example, "Sneakers."
3. Click post.

After you have uploaded your campaign, go immediately to your Google AdWords account. You will find your new campaign added with all of the specific criteria defined. *Always* check your campaign. I like to ensure that everything has been uploaded properly and that my daily budget and targeting preferences have been entered correctly. On one occasion my daily max and targeting criteria were not set correctly, and it cost me quite a few dollars. Don't let this happen to you! Click on the campaign and verify the posted information below the heading at the top of your page. Make any necessary corrections before logging out of Google AdWords and the AdWords Editor.

What's great about the editor is that you can also import data from your online AdWords account. This comes in handy after you've launched your campaign and want to optimize it. For example, as mentioned earlier, I like to have my ads in positions 3–8. This helps to lower costs and improve conversions.

To manage this effectively without spending a lot of time on it, each week after I launch my campaign, I update my Google AdWords Editor to display ad position and adjust my bids. You can sort your data every which way to Sunday to make this process as simple as possible and upload your changes easily.

As you become more familiar with the Editor, you'll discover a variety of ways it can help you launch a new campaign, as well as manage existing promotions and access retired ones.

Chapter Summary

- Use Google AdWords Editor to upload your offline campaigns and manage large keyword lists.

- Create a new campaign by selecting Daily Budget/Campaign, Ad Groups, Ads, and Keywords. Each campaign will have one unique keyword and two unique ads per ad group (broad, phrase, and match).

  Keywords first. Create the following columns:

  - Campaign name (must be the same down the whole column)
  - Ad groups
  - Keywords
  - Match Type X3 (broad, phrase, and exact)
  - =PROPER (A2) will capitalize

  Ad groups

  - List the campaign name (same as above) and same for each ad group
  - Ad group name, which will be the same as your ad title but can be longer as there is not the same twenty-five-character limit
  - Bids (What is the amount that you want to bid? I like to start at between $0.50 and $1.00. Make sure your decimals are in the right place!)
  - =PROPER (A2) will provide initial caps

Ads

- Each ad will have the keyword in the heading
- Campaign column (same spelling as other spreadsheets)
- Ad groups (just paste the ones you created)
- Headline (use =PROPER (A2) to capitalize the words)
- Copy and paste to get rid of the formula
- Sort by text length (make sure to select both columns)
- Add negative keywords. Excluding irrelevant keywords improves click-through rate (CTR), which improves quality score.
- Always keep benefit to one line (X2)

Budget management

- AdWords budget should be less than $100/week to start. Once a campaign is starting to generate clicks and conversions, double your spend each week until you've optimized your returns.

Visit http://MyPPCmadesimple.com/secret to compare keyword tools: Keywords Spy costs around $100 per month depending on the package you choose. Others like KeyCompete cost around $300/year.

VII. A Focus on Budget

Budgeting is an important aspect of effective pay-per-click marketing. Many of the companies I've consulted for have told me about their struggles with PPC budgets. When I ask them how much they spend, they often tell me around $5,000 per month. Then I asked them what type of return they get, and I see a few blank stares or receive semi-incoherent responses. There's no reason whatsoever to spend more than two or three hundred dollars on PPC before making it profitable or moving on.

Unfortunately, it's not uncommon to hear about companies or individuals spending large sums of money on unprofitable PPC campaigns. They often think that eventually the clicks will turn into customers. I have found with pay-per-click advertising that there is a very short half-life. This means that if your clicks don't turn into conversions of some kind (purchase, opt-in, sign up, etc.) within forty-eight to seventy-two hours, the likelihood of conversion is nonexistent. Personally, if I'm not making money after spending a couple of hundred bucks, I turn my campaigns off. I don't understand the logic of scaling an unprofitable campaign and expecting it to somehow become profitable.

Achieving improved conversion rates is all about choosing the right keywords, writing powerful ads, and having pages that convert. Add the right budgeting techniques and you're sure to win! Here are a few of the techniques I use to ensure success with new and existing campaigns.

1. **Decide what you can afford.** The first step is to set a budget that you're comfortable with and stick to it. When you're first starting out with pay-per-click advertising, it's easy to keep throwing money at a campaign wishing and hoping until you get your first sale. But I think that spending $300 to get a $30 sale is just crazy. You wouldn't spend ten times more than you have to on anything else, so why treat online advertising any differently?

   For each new campaign, set a total budget (i.e., "I'm going to spend $100–$200 to promote this product and see if I can sell it") and a daily budget. Your daily budget can be as little as $5 - $10/day or as much as the value of your total budget. Personally, I like to let my campaigns run for at least five days if not a full week when trying something new. Take your total spend and divide by seven to get a daily budget amount when launching a brand new campaign.

2. **Determine your budget by the number of keywords you have.** How do you know what your budget should be? There's no hard-and-fast rule on budgeting. However, a guideline I like to use is a maximum of $10/day for each grouping of fifty keywords. That way, if you start your campaign with around one hundred keywords, you're spending $20/day. In five days, your total spend is $100. This math is easy to follow and is enough of a budget to get you clicks. By tracking which

keywords are producing the greatest number of clicks and conversions, you can target your increased spend appropriately.

3. **Increase your budget on profitable keywords.** Once you have launched your campaign and started to see activity, pay close attention to which keywords are generating sales for you. If your tracking is in place, then you'll know where you want to focus your budget. Converting keywords should get 80 percent of your budget. Why not 100 percent? Because you should always be experimenting with new keywords and phrases— expanding your list over time. Remember, in most instances we only started with one hundred keywords. Successful PPC marketers add hundreds if not thousands of keywords to their campaigns to find additional high-converting keywords or phrases.

   To get the most from your winning keywords, increase your daily spend. A great way to do this is to create a new campaign that includes your winning keywords only. This lets you manage your winners with a single budget. Unfortunately, this can impact your quality score at first, but having all the winners in a single campaign more than makes up for it. Again, the key is focusing your budget on keywords that convert. Keep that in mind and you'll always have profitable campaigns.

Start small and build up to larger budgets. The mistake many online markets make when starting with PPC is that they believe that more spend is better. The truth is that the right spend, small or large, is what's most important.

Chapter Summary
• Budgeting is an important aspect of effective pay-per-click marketing.

• Decide what you can afford to spend on your new PPC campaign before you begin.

• Determine your budget based upon how many keywords you have. $5 - $10/day for each grouping of fifty keywords.

• Increase your budget on profitable keywords, adding and trying new keywords on a regular basis.

VIII. Google Quality Score

So we've touched on quality score a couple of times and discussed various methods for improving your campaigns. Now it's time to discuss the importance of Quality Score in relation to running profitable Google AdWords campaigns. Quality Score is calculated by a formula that considers click-through rate, relevance, bid price, and landing page quality.

It has been reported that click-through-rate is the most heavily weighted factor when determining Quality Score. As a result, you should focus on generating and testing compelling ads.

After Google has determined your Quality Score, it uses this value in a variety of ways to insure a positive user experience. Some ways Quality Score is used include the following:

- influencing your keywords' actual cost-per-clicks (CPCs)
- estimating the first page bids that you see in your account
- determining if a keyword is eligible to enter the ad auction that occurs when a user enters a search query
- affecting how high your ad will be ranked

Remember that in both organic search as well as pay per click, Google is looking to deliver quality results. To do so, they use the Quality Score to determine just how relevant your ads are to each search query.

Want your ad to appear higher on the page and pay less for it? Improving your Quality Score can help. Quality Score measures how relevant ads and keywords are to search queries. Because Google wants the most relevant ads to place high on the page, they take both your bid amount and your Quality Score into account when determining where your ad is positioned. Your ad rank can be calculated with a simple formula (Ad Rank = CPC bid × Quality Score).

If Google didn't have Quality Score, then whoever bid the most, no matter how relevant the ad was to the search, would appear on top. This would be a bad experience for searchers, because they wouldn't see the most relevant ads for their search, and it would be inefficient for advertisers, because they would be paying for clicks that are unlikely to convert. Using Quality Score allows Google to reward relevant ads with higher placement and lower first page bid estimates.

How Is Quality Score Calculated?

A Quality Score is calculated for each keyword in your account and weighs:

- Your keyword's historical click-through rate (CTR)

- The relevance of your keyword to the ads in its ad group

- The relevance of your keyword and ad to the user's search query

- The relevance of your keyword to your landing page

Where Can You Find Your Quality Score?

To view the Quality Score of your keywords, click on the magnifying glass next to each keyword. Clicking on the details and recommendations link shown underneath your Quality Score will provide more information on your score and how you can improve it. You can also see the quality score of your ads by clicking the "Keywords" tab. From there, select "customize columns" at the top of the ad group table. Select "Show Quality Score" from the drop-down menu. Click "Done" when you're finished. Each keyword's Quality Score will be described as a number out of 10 possible points. A quality score of 10/10 is the best and 0/10, the worst. Strive for a minimum quality of 5/10 and an average of 7/10 or better.

How Do You Get a High Quality Score?

1. Your keywords and ads must relate to each other. Include your keywords in your ads when possible. In addition to the ad writing strategies we've deployed so far, consider going further and customizing one of the ads for each keyword. For example, if your keyword is running shoes, the corresponding ad should mention running shoes.

2. Group similar keywords together. An ad group consists of a couple of ads and a single keyword (or set of keywords) that will trigger those ads. Because the same ads will appear for any keyword in an ad group, it's best to group keywords by theme, so that you can write more targeted ads.

3. Create landing pages relevant to your keywords and ads. If you are bidding on the term "running shoes," then the page your ad links to should NOT contain information about blue sweaters. Rather, it should be consistent with the subject matter of your ad.

4. Keywords should be relevant to your customers. The more relevant your keywords are to those you're targeting, the more likely customers are to click on your ad. Put yourself in the shoes of your customers and imagine the keywords they would type into Google when they're looking for your product or service. This is why the keyword research we do early on is so important. More targeted keywords will generate fewer impressions, but they are more likely to lead to sales and have a higher CTR.

Quality Score Optimization Tips

To improve quality score, ask yourself if your AdWords campaign meets the following criteria.

Keywords. Do your keywords…

- Include terms specific to your business?
- Relate to your ad group and landing page?
- Include synonyms and alternate spellings?
- Include negative keywords?

Ads. Do your ads…

- Include a keyword in your headline?
- Clearly explain what you offer?

- Include a call-to-action phrase (like "Order Today")?
- Point to a landing page that most represents the ad text?

Test at least two ads per ad group. Delete or edit ads with a low CTR. Continue to test and refine your ads.

Account Structure. Does each campaign…

- Relate to one product or theme?
- Include multiple, tightly knit ad groups, each containing a list of keywords sharing a common theme?
- Target the right location and language in which you provide services?
- Avoid duplicate keywords across ad groups?

Create separate campaigns for Search and the Content Network.

You might be asking, why spend so much time on quality score? There are essentially two reasons why quality score is so important. The first is related to traffic and the second to conversions (a.k.a. money). Reason one is that by formatting your ads properly, you're going to get good click-through rates from browsers you want. If you're not paying attention, others competing for the same audience are going to be generating site visits and you won't—it's as simple as that. The second reason is that quality score is a measure of the overall purchase process you're offering to future customers. Google not only considers the relevancy of your ads but also landing pages. They want to make sure that Google browsers have a consistent and positive user experience. This only happens when the keyword, ad, and landing page are consistent. By paying attention to your quality score, you can manipulate different campaign elements that guarantee a positive user experience, resulting in higher clicks and conversions.

To see quality score:

The Quality Score column displays your keyword's Quality Score to help you monitor its performance. This column is disabled by default in new accounts, but you can make it show in your account statistics by following these steps:

1. Sign in to your AdWords account at https://adwords.google.com.
2. Select the campaign and ad group for which you'd like to see keyword Quality Scores.
3. Select the Keywords tab.
4. Click Filters and Views, and then Customize columns at the top of the ad group table.
5. Check Quality Score from the options that appear.
6. Click Save to hide the drop-down menu again.

Chapter Summary

- Quality Score is calculated by a formula that considers click-through rate, relevance, bid price, and landing page quality.

- It has been reported that click-through-rate is the most heavily weighted factor when determining Quality Score.

- Quality score is used to influence keywords' cost-per-click, estimate first page bids, determine if a keyword is eligible to enter the ad auction, and affects how high your ad will be ranked

- Quality score is calculated through multiple factors including CTR and relevance.

- To view the Quality Score of your keywords, click on the magnifying glass next to each keyword.

- To get a high quality score: relate keywords and ads to each other, group similar keywords together, create relevant landing pages, and use relevant keywords.

- Optimize quality score using the tips noted in this chapter.

IX. Landing Page Optimization

All of your effort to produce a well-structured AdWords campaign is meaningless unless you develop high-converting landing pages. Keep in mind that even the best landing pages are useless if you're not delivering the right type of traffic. I consider the right kind of traffic to be browsers who intend to take an action. This is why it's important to use the Microsoft Commercial Intent tool when doing keyword research.

Another way to think about it is through the lens of segmentation. The people buying the products or services you offer have a specific need. If your product solves that need for them, they should know about it. By writing your ads for those in need and having an emotional appeal, you can motivate prospects to take action even before reaching your landing page.

After working within Google AdWords to optimize your campaign and get really targeted ads, the next step is to focus on landing page optimization. A question I often get is whether or not someone needs to create one hundred landing pages for one hundred keywords. You can rest easy because the answer to that question is no. However, to improve conversion rates, you may consider having more than one landing page. To avoid having to create tons of landing pages, I group my keywords (on a separate spreadsheet) to determine appropriate destination URLs/landing pages I need to develop.

Here's the good news. In my experience, you only need a small handful of landing pages, and they don't have to be all that different. In fact, by just updating your meta tags and the headline, you can improve quality score and conversion. So when I talk about creating unique landing pages, keep in mind that I'm referring to minor changes on pages that generally look and feel the same.

Another tactic I use is to create "themed" landing pages. These pages are designed to include more than one product or service offering. This is ideal because it limits the number of landing pages that need to be developed while at the same time improving click-through rates. A good example would be a site that focuses on selling cameras.

The main page can be used for more generic PPC ads focused on cameras whereas the camera listing pages would work well for any PPC ads promoting specific digital cameras. The actual camera description pages should be used when promoting specific cameras in this example. The more targeted you make your ads, the higher the conversion rate.

Essentially, you want to make different landing pages for different ad groups when the keywords being targeted are thematically different. For example, create unique landing pages for ad groups covering "digital cameras" keywords and for "digital SLR camera" keywords. This goes back to what we talked about earlier regarding relevancy. The more relevant your ad is to what browsers will find when they hit your landing page, the better the quality score.

What makes a good landing page? From my perspective, the best landing pages:

- Are well formatted. They have your keyword(s) in the domain (if possible), meta tags, and page headings. In the meta tags and the meta description of the page, add keywords similar to your ad campaign, and in the description part put content similar to your PPC ads in general. In Google's eyes, this indicates ads that are very relevant to your target landing page. That's big bonus points when it comes to the landing page score!
- Easy navigation. It's best to have at least four pages but usually more, in addition to the actual landing page. These pages should be accessible from the main navigation of your home page. This gives the site content that improves quality score and builds credibility.

- Have a layout that makes your offer simple to take advantage of (click here, buy now, etc.). If possible, place your offer above the fold. When browsers don't have to scroll to see your offer, conversions increase.
- Highlight the benefits of the offer. Avoid overcrowding. Keep your landing pages clean and simple. Black type on a white background work best.
- Focuses on the emotional aspects of the target audience.
- Have the presence of sales page factors like testimonials, "as seen on TV," images, and emotional appeal.
- Minimize distraction. Clean navigation and very few options for leaving the page.
- Strong call to action. Green buttons work best.

This may look simple, but that's the point of this book. These factors are based on more than a decade of experience, lots of testing, and a ton of money spent on pay-per-click marketing campaigns. This is important because a good landing page score means higher relevancy scores and lower PPC costs.

I spent many years looking for the perfect landing page template, one that I could simply use each time I wanted to start a new Google AdWords campaign. The challenge is that each offer is unique, and landing pages need to work in conjunction with your Web site. If marketing affiliate products, this may not be the case, and using something like WordPress templates may be an option. Regardless, I have found that my best-performing landing pages are those I copied from others and modified to meet my specific needs.

If you don't have design skills or find the process of landing page development too difficult, I recommend finding someone to partner with. Use Elance.com, oDesk, or GetAFreelancer.com to recruit a designer with landing page development experience. You can even recruit a copywriter if you want to outsource the entire project. But don't leave it up to chance. Even if you're working with someone, use the list above to ensure that all of the necessary criteria have been met.

Using the example we discussed earlier, let's assume that we are going to be launching our "Sneakers" campaign. I would first group the keywords into logical groupings. For example if we have sneaker-related keywords, like "running shoes," "runner shoe," "runner shoes," etc., taking visitors to a page that focuses on shoes for runners will improve quality score and conversions. Sending the same users to a page focused on everything under the sun— men's shoes, dress shoes, high-heeled shoes, etc.—would make for a bad user experience and very low conversion.

The lesson to learn is that you really benefit by putting yourself in the customer's shoes. Regardless of what you're selling, you must consider the complete user experience from search query to ad to landing page. Do your best to make this experience seamless and you will see strong results.

The only other important aspect of landing page development is the offer. I have spent a lot of time building and promoting Web pages and landing pages and an equal amount of time driving traffic to them. However, if an offer isn't well developed, your conversions can never be at their highest. What do I mean when I say offer?

- 14 Day Free Trial
- Save 10%
- Limited Quantity. Act Now!
- Buy One, Get One

You need to devise an offer that works for your business. And don't interpret the concept of an offer as a discount. Some of the most popular offers include access to videos or instructional guides that enhance the overall value of the purchase. The point I'm trying to make here is that after the headline, your offer is the most important thing on the page. Spend time developing your offers and testing them. This is also the benefit of having multiple landing pages in rotation. Test multiple offers to see which one generates the highest conversion.

A Better Way to Dramatically Improve Conversion Rates

Even though I've been engaged in online marketing for more than a dozen years, it never ceases to amaze me just how little I know about online behavior. I've often created the "perfect" landing page only to find conversions sluggish. How can this be? I've created a consistent user experience, have a great headline and strong call to action, designed the page aesthetically, but still poor results.

Enter yet another Google tool called Web Site Optimizer. You can access this tool through Google Webmaster Tools at http://webmaster.google.com or simply typing "Webmaster tools" into the Google search engine. There you can find a variety of helpful resources including the Google Web Site Optimizer.

The tool allows you to rotate different landing pages on autopilot without having to change the destination URLs that are contained within your ads. Perhaps you want to try a different headline, change the color of your "buy now" button, or test a completely different layout. The Web Site Optimizer lets you rotate these pages—no matter how similar or different—using the same Web site address.

Chapter Summary

- After working within Google AdWords to optimize your campaign and get really targeted ads, the next step is to focus on landing page optimization.

- You can improve your quality score and conversion rates by creating themed landing pages.

- Good landing pages are well formatted, provide easy navigation, and have visible offers.

- To improve landing page effectiveness highlight benefits and focus on the emotion appeal. Include sales page identifiers, minimize distractions, and have a strong call to action.

- Use Elance.com, oDesk, or GetAFreelancer.com to recruit a designer with landing page development experience.

- A key element of any successful landing page is the offer.

- Sign up for Google Web Site Optimizer to improve the effectiveness of your landing page.

- Google Web Site Optimizer allows you to rotate different landing pages on autopilot without having to change the destination URL – measuring the effectiveness of landing page components.

X. Tracking Performance

One of the best features of Google AdWords is the ability to track performance. The large majority of you reading this book will be selling your own products and services, and others may be more interested in making a living through affiliate marketing. Regardless of your desire, tracking is available to help analyze the effectiveness of your campaigns. I will discuss tracking using Google Conversion tracking and Google Analytics as well as alternate options for those engaged in affiliate marketing.

Tracking your campaigns is essential for managing your spend and ensuring a positive return on your investment (ROI). If your costs exceed your revenue, you can manipulate your campaign to reduce expenses. Conversely, if your campaign is making money, you can increase your spend on converting keywords. To manage your campaigns in this way, you need a clear understanding of what's working and what isn't.

If you are promoting your own product or service, Google makes it *really* easy to track your campaign's effectiveness. Here's how it works. First, by using the Google AdWords interface, you have instant access to how your ads are performing. This includes the number of impressions of your ads, top keywords, click-through rates, and even quality score. This provides a good understanding of which keywords and ads are generating activity, but what happens after the click? This is where Google Analytics and Google Conversion Tracking come in.

As a best practice, I always include Google Analytics on my Web pages and landing pages. The analytics provide a great deal of valuable information and have recently become more integrated with Google Conversion Tracking. In essence, I use every type of tracking Google provides because I want to know which keywords are generating the greatest response. By doing so, I can spend less and make more.

I consider Google AdWords Conversion Tracking to be the magic bullet. Conversion Tracking is a free tool offered by Google to help you measure conversions and identify how effective your AdWords ads and keywords are.

By placing a small piece of code on your "Thank you page" (the page users see after making a purchase), you can trace which keywords and ads generated actual conversions. This is a must-have for people promoting their own products and services. By knowing which keywords are generating the greatest conversions, you can spend more to generate additional traffic that converts. Alternatively, you can shut off the keywords that are generating a lot of clicks but little or no conversions. Why spend the money if all you're doing is shelling out cash and getting nothing in return?

If you're using the AdWords conversion tracking tool, clicks originating on Google.com and selected Google Network sites will be tracked. In combination with Google Analytics, both tracking mechanisms help you to better understand the path of prospects who convert into paying customers. This can help you better understand the elements of the purchase funnel and make appropriate changes to your landing pages or Web site.

How to Add Google Conversion Tracking to Your Web Site

To begin using conversion tracking, you must first put the AdWords Conversion Tracking code onto your site. This basic code is provided to you once you sign up for AdWords Conversion Tracking. Even if you don't know a lot about Web site programming, you probably know how to cut and paste text. If you can, you can set this up on your own by taking the code provided and pasting it onto your Web pages. You'll need a Web editor of sorts, but this is usually provided by whoever is hosting your site or can be done using a tool like Dreamweaver or FrontPage.

Some people I've worked with have been concerned about placing tracking code on their site and its impact on page load. Conversion tracking will not affect how fast your Web pages load. The tracking code happens so quickly that there is no performance impact to your Web site. Performance is compromised when you have lots of different tracking mechanisms on a single page and it has to make multiple calls to numerous servers. Stick with Google Conversion Tracking and you won't be impacted.

How Does the Tracking Code Actually Work?

Once your tracking code is correctly applied, AdWords Conversion Tracking will place a cookie on a user's computer or mobile device when he or she clicks on one of your AdWords ads. Then, if the user reaches one of your conversion pages, the cookie is connected to your Web page. When a match is made, Google records a successful conversion for you. The cookie Google adds to a user's computer or portable device when he or she clicks on an ad expires in approximately thirty days. This is pretty common for Web site cookies and essentially means that if someone clicks on an ad and purchases within a thirty-day period, the two will be connected. Some browsers don't want to be tracked. As a result, they can choose not to participate in tracking via Internet browser settings. These users will simply not be included in your conversion tracking statistics.

What Can You Track with This Code?

When using conversion tracking, you can set up to thirty customized names for your actions. You can then organize actions into categories by using the following labels. This helps you clearly understand what you're tracking and simplifies the overall tracking process.

Purchases/sales. The most common form of tracking, purchases/sales helps you track purchases through your Web site—initiating from a Google AdWords click (I told you that Conversion Tracking was awesome). This tracking determines your return on investment (ROI) and can even provide insight into the path buyers take from click to purchase. The purchase is often tracked by the "Thank you" page. This is because anyone who reaches that particular page on your Web site would have to pass through and successfully purchase.

Leads. You might not be selling directly based on your AdWords campaign. You may be running a two-step promotion or perhaps want to generate leads for offline conversion. A good example of this would be a realtor looking to find people who want to buy a new home. They aren't going to buy the house online but can certainly raise their hand indicating a high level of interest in using your services. Once individuals submit their contact information, the page they see may say something like "Thank you for contacting us." In this case, you are tracking everyone who clicks on your PPC ad and arrives at the "Thank you" page successfully.

Sign-ups. A number of Web sites offer some type of sign up giving users access to subscriptions, newsletters, or downloads. It's common for users to arrive at a page that says "Your subscription has been processed" once the submission process is complete.

Views of a key page. This aspect of tracking helps Web sites track the number of times users have landed on a single page that's important to your business. This may be a review page or services page that identifies what you offer or focuses on a specific promotion. In essence, it's any important page of your Web site that you want users to view.

Other. The final option of "other" tracks a category unique to your service or business. This is an ideal option for unique businesses that are testing new campaigns or an action that doesn't fall into one of the previous categories mentioned.

What Happens When You Can't Install Conversion Tracking?

If you are promoting an affiliate product, you might be wondering how you can track conversions. Unfortunately, Google Conversion Tracking isn't going to help much. Rather, you'll need to rely on the affiliate tracking system to analyze your performance. Often times I use affiliate tracking codes that allow for the use of a variable.

I'll be covering this process in future publications, but essentially you need to set up a numbering system that allows you to identify keywords by tracking URL. A great example would be a product that I'm promoting from ClickBank, a popular affiliate marketing aggregator. The tracking URL looks something like this, http://mfleisch9.bryxen1.hop.clickbank.net/?tid=31. When a sale happens, I can access (via ClickBank) the referring URL. Because I have a unique URL (i.e., number) for each keyword, I know that #31 refers to the keyword "SEO Elite Offer." The trick is that each affiliate tracking system is a little different, so you'll need to do your research and customize your AdWord destination URLs appropriately.

Again, use the Google AdWords Editor to create a long list of unique identifiers or code by hand. I also recommend checking out Tracking202. This is a great tracking tool that is often used by affiliate marketers and doesn't require code to be place on conversion pages. It provides a simple way to track, monitor, and calculate all your PPC accounts and campaigns. When you have multiple PPC accounts and campaigns running, effectively managing them can be a tedious task. What's more, tracking converting keywords vs. non-converting keywords can require custom programming or expensive software that isn't intuitive or user friendly. Tracking202 does a great job of automating the tracking process.

The tool provides real-time tracking that gives up-to-the-second data on all your active PPC accounts and provides easy to read graphs, automatic keyword trackers, and automated profit calculations. This can save you tons of time and help you to better understand which campaigns and keywords are producing a positive ROI.

Getting Technical: How AdWords Conversion Tracking Actually Works

Once you've defined an action, Google gives you a JavaScript snippet to paste on the pages you wish to track. This code builds a URL that passes parameters back to Google and also allows you to display the Google Site Stats text on your page if you opted in to show it on your conversion pages. The query string data within the JavaScript code snippet is used in the following way:

- **Google_conversion_id**: A unique value that allows Google to identify the advertiser receiving the conversion.
- **Google_conversion_value**: A numeric value defined by the advertiser equaling the value of the conversion.
- **Google_conversion_label**: The type of conversion that occurred (purchase, sign-up, page view, or lead). Google does not currently support advertiser-

defined conversion types. Consequently, you cannot customize this string.

- **Google_conversion_language**: The language of the conversion tracking Google Site Stats text that appears on your Web site.

Proper installation of the code on to your site activates conversion tracking. Here's how it should behave once it starts working:

1. A user clicks your AdWords ad.
2. A Google server places a temporary cookie on the user's computer or portable device.
3. If the user reaches one of your designated conversion confirmation request pages, his or her computer passes back the cookie and requests that the Google server send the conversion tracking text information. If cookies are rejected for any reason, the conversions made from that user won't be recorded. Conversion tracking is also not supported if the user disables cookies or images.
4. Google records the conversion event and correlates it with your campaign, ad group, URL, and keyword.
5. On your report you will see conversion statistics from the campaign level down to the keyword level.

How Conversion Tracking Works with Google Analytics

As I mentioned earlier, Google AdWords Conversion Tracking and Google Analytics work really well together.

AdWords advertisers with linked AdWords accounts who have opted into Data Sharing can import Analytics data into AdWords Conversion Tracking. Some of the benefits of using conversion tracking with Analytics are:

- Convenient access to Analytics goals, transactions, and session data related to your AdWords ad clicks.
- AdWords conversions and Analytics goals and transactions displayed alongside each other so you can spot further opportunities to optimize your advertising campaigns. Although advertisers must link Analytics data to AdWords Conversion Tracking in order to see these stats, you do not need to tag any Analytics conversion pages with the AdWords Conversion Tracking code.
- Google Analytics data is automatically imported into the Conversion Optimizer to streamline bidding for conversions at a lower cost. The Conversion Optimizer optimizes your placement in the ad auction to make sure you get low-converting clicks only if they are cheap while still getting you as many high-converting clicks as possible.

You must have a Google Analytics account in order to link the two features. My recommendation is to use each independently first. By doing so you can learn the features and benefits that each one has to offer. After running your campaigns for a couple of months and seeing the type of data each one provides, you can then merge your accounts.

The Benefits of Conversion Tracking

When you have access to conversion data in your reports, you can make smarter online advertising decisions, particularly about what ads and keywords you invest in. Given better data, you can measure your overall return on investment (ROI) for your AdWords campaigns more effectively.

For example, let's say that you own a business that sells suitcases online. You know how many clicks your AdWords campaign gets, but would like to know specifically which keywords are converting to sales. With basic conversion tracking, you can get this valuable information. With customized conversion tracking, you can also report the dollar amount of each sale and get the total revenue generated by each of his keywords as compared to the total cost of the keyword.

With conversion statistics, you discover that the keyword "travel suitcase" has a return on investment (ROI) of 500 percent. Consequently, you optimize your campaign by increasing the spending on that keyword, maximizing your AdWords return on investment.

AdWords Conversion Tracking Setup

Conversion tracking involves placing a cookie on a user's computer when he or she clicks on an ad. Then, if someone clicks on your ad and reaches one of your conversion pages, the user's browser sends the cookie to a Google server, and a small conversion-tracking image is displayed on your site. When such a match is made, Google records a successful conversion for you. This information is presented within the "Campaigns," "Conversion Tracking," or "Report Center" sections in your AdWords account.

Implementing conversion tracking is simple: place a few lines of code, referred to as a "code snippet," on your Web site pages. As a prerequisite, you or someone in your organization must have a working knowledge of HTML or Web tools in order to successfully place the conversion tracking code snippet. You'll also need to have access to your Web site's code and the Google AdWords account that corresponds to the site.

Once you have successfully installed your code snippet, you can access your conversion tracking reports from the Campaigns page, Conversions page, and the Report Center at least one hour after the first conversion from your AdWords account. You will even be able to see conversion reports down to the keyword level.

Note: If you believe that you do not have the requisite knowledge to successfully implement Google's conversion tracking, outsource the task to a qualified developer at Elance.com. I've found many qualified individuals to handle my programming tasks for me using this site, which provides access to thousands of qualified designers and programmers.

Getting the Code Snippet
When the code snippet is placed on the conversion page of your Web site, statistics on users who click on a Google

AdWords ad and complete a conversion (purchase, sign-up, page view, or lead) can be collected and viewed on your conversion tracking reports.

The Google code snippet is provided when you sign up from the Conversions page located under the Reporting tab in your AdWords account. This code snippet is very basic but can successfully track conversions when placed on your conversion page(s) mentioned previously.

Purchase Conversion Default: Sample Code Only—DO NOT USE

```
<!-- Google Code for Purchase Conversion Page -->
<script language="JavaScript" type="text/javascript">
<!--
var google_conversion_id = 1234567890;
var google_conversion_language = "en_US";
var google_conversion_format = "1";
var google_conversion_color = "666666";
var google_conversion_label = "Purchase";
//-->
</script>
<script language="JavaScript"
src="http://www.googleadservices.com/pagead/conversion.
js">
</script>
<noscript>
<img height=1 width=1 border=0
src="http://www.googleadservices.com/pagead/conversion/
1234567890/?value=1&label=Purchas
e&script=0">
</noscript>
```

Requirements

The only requirements for installing conversion tracking on your Web site are as follows:

- AdWords ads that are approved and running
- Placement of the Google code snippet on the conversion page

There are no specific system requirements for your customers. For AdWords Conversion Tracking to properly track conversions from clicks on your ad, customers must be able to download images and enable the "cookies" feature in their browsers. Although this is the default setting for most Web browsers, users who don't accept the conversion tracking cookies won't be included in your statistics.

Inserting the Code Snippet on Your Web Site

To properly track a conversion, the code snippet should be placed between the <body> tags, closer to the </body> tag so that the image appears further down the page. You should NOT place the code in the header or footer of your page. This could overstate your conversion statistics and defeat the purpose of tracking.

Once your code is placed, you should start seeing stats in short order. Google professes the code will begin collecting information in about an hour after installation and promotion. If you see conversions on your Web site regularly, you should begin to see the conversion tracking working the same day it's implemented.

Remember that the reason you went through the trouble of placing your inclusion tracking code was to determine which keywords and ads are generating a positive return on your investment. I've spent a good deal of time explaining how to implement tracking because it's one of the most important aspects of running effective PPC campaigns. I personally found the whole concept of tracking a bit daunting at first, but it gets easier with time.

Once you have all the data, it's time to determine which campaigns are effective and which are not. Let's talk about measuring your return on investment (ROI) or as I like to call it, *profit,* in the next chapter.

Chapter Summary

- Tracking your campaigns is essential for managing your spend and ensuring a positive return on your AdWords investment.

- As a best practice, include Google Analytics on your Web pages and landing pages.

- Conversion Tracking is a free tool offered by Google to help you measure conversions and identify the effectiveness of your AdWords ads and keywords.

- If you're using the AdWords conversion tracking tool, clicks originating on Google.com and selected Google Network sites will be tracked.

- To begin using conversion tracking, you must first put the AdWords Conversion Tracking code on your Web site.

- When a user clicks on your ad, Google conversion tracking tracks the click through to a conversion.

- When using conversion tracking, you can set up to thirty customized names to track specific actions you want to track: Purchases/sales, leads, sign ups, page views, and other.

- Use Tracking202 to effectively analyze affiliate marketing campaigns.

- A description of how AdWords conversion tracking works from a technical perspective was provided as well as how it works with Google Analytics.

- When you have access to conversion data in your reports, you can make smarter online advertising decisions, particularly about what ads and keywords you spend your money on.

- An explanation of how to add Google Conversion Tracking to your website is provided.

XI. Measuring ROI

If you've launched your first campaign, you probably already reviewed the number of clicks and impressions your ads receive, but are you tracking your return on investment (ROI) too?

Tracking your ROI can help you answer questions like: Which keywords give me the most profit? How can I improve my campaign's performance? Just think of ROI as a measure of how profitable your campaigns and keywords actually are. You can compare your ROI for your campaigns on a regular basis to track your profitability. You want to find the campaigns that generate a profit and increase the level of traffic you're sending to them.

The first step to calculating ROI is to identify and measure your conversions. A conversion can be any event that you want a customer to complete, such as a purchase, lead submission, or account sign-up. To track conversions, you can use the AdWords Conversion Tracking tool (check out the link at the top of your AdWords account menu), or you can simply add up the dollars generated from your AdWords traffic on your own (how many sales or other conversions you received from people who clicked on AdWords ads). Obviously, I recommend installing the conversion tracking code because it's easy to do and will give you accurate information.

After you identify your conversions, you can calculate your ROI with one of the formulas shown below. The simple calculation for ROI is your profit divided by the amount you spend on AdWords. This formula can be applied to your entire account, one specific campaign, or even a keyword. It all depends on how detailed your conversion measurement statistics are.

Formula for Sales: Revenue of items sold – cost of goods sold (production costs, cost to advertise items on AdWords, and related expenses) = ROI

Formula for conversions other than sales: Dollar value of all leads, sign-ups, or other conversions - cost to advertise on AdWords = ROI.

If you have an ROI that's greater than one (or 100 percent), then your advertising is profitable. For example, if your ROI = 2 (or 200 percent), then you are generating $2 in profit for every $1 in advertising that you spend.

How does knowing your ROI help make you more profitable? Here's an example: Let's say an advertiser has two keywords ("roses" and "carnations") and spends $50 on each. Because the two keywords have different average costs-per-click (CPCs), for the same $50, the advertiser received fifty clicks for "roses" and one hundred clicks for "carnations."

Keywords	Impressn	Clicks	Cost	Avg. CPC	Conv	Profit	ROI
roses	1,000	50	$50	$1.00	5	?	?
carnations	1,000	100	$50	$0.50	10	?	?

You can get all of the information in this table in your own account except for profit and ROI, which you will have to calculate yourself. Based on this data, the keyword "carnations" seems like the better of the two because it has a lower average CPC and it leads to more conversions (in this case sales of flowers). But without tracking the ROI on both keywords, we can't know for sure which is more profitable. Now let's look at the data with ROI and profit filled in.

Keywords	Impressions	Clicks	Cost	Avg. CPC	Conversions	Profit	ROI
roses	1,000	50	$50	$1.00	5	$100	200%
carnations	1,000	100	$50	$0.50	10	75	150%

The ROI for "roses" is 200 percent ($100 profit/$50 cost). The ROI for "carnations" is 150 percent ($75 profit/$50 cost). Notice that the keyword "roses" has a higher profit and much better ROI, even though it generated fewer conversions and clicks. This could be the case for a variety of reasons—for example, users who clicked on the "roses" ad may tend to buy more expensive products or be more prone to purchase than those search on "carnations." Additionally, products are priced differently.

So even though "roses" has a higher average CPC and receives fewer conversions, it makes more money than "carnations." Therefore, it makes sense to pay more for "roses" because it has a higher ROI and gives you more profit.

When you track and monitor your ROI, you can make smarter decisions about your online ads and, ultimately, make your business more profitable. To accurately determine your ROI, you must first determine how to accurately track your conversions and use your ROI data to properly manage your AdWords account. Essentially, what you need to know is how often clicks convert into customers and how much profit you make on each AdWords-generated lead or conversion. To determine this number, you must track how many customers you get directly from AdWords itself.

There are a couple of methods you can use to track leads and conversion through Google AdWords. My favorite method is using the Google AdWords Conversion Tracking tool, but you can also use your own tracking code, or a third-party tracking system like Tracking 202. What's nice about a tool like Tracking 202 is that you can track all of your PPC campaigns from a single place regardless of where you're running them (Yahoo, Bing, etc.).

Right now, let's focus on the Google AdWords Conversion Tracking, which can show you exactly which keywords are generating conversions. Remember, a conversion doesn't necessarily have to be a sale; it can be any type of transaction, including signups, downloads, or clicks of a certain kind.

Setting Up and Using Conversion Tracking Effectively

As we discussed in a previous section, setting up and installing Google Conversion Tracking is easy. All you need to do is place a few lines of code on your Web pages, and presto! Placing the code takes some basic knowledge of HTML. You'll also need to have access to your Web site's code and the Google AdWords account that corresponds to the site.

When accessing your AdWords account, click on the Reporting tab. There you will be able to select "conversions." The first time you visit the page, it may provide you with the code needed to place on your Web pages. If not, simply click the "new conversion" button and follow the on-screen instructions. Once you have successfully installed your conversion tracking code, you can access your conversion tracking reports from the Report Center at least one hour after the first conversion from your AdWords account. You will even be able to see conversion reports down to the keyword level.

When setting up conversion tracking, you can add what the conversion means to you from a financial perspective (ex: profit). This will help you track your ROI. If you enter "Revenue for your conversion" you can then find your ROI by running an Account, Campaign, Ad Group, or Keyword Performance report in your AdWords Report Center. Click "save and get code" to access the code snippet to be added to your Web site.

Once you place the code on your Web site, and most importantly your thank you pages, campaign data becomes truly effective and can help you quickly determine your most profitable keywords.

Using Your ROI Data

Whenever your ROI is more than 100 percent, you're doing well and making money from your online advertising campaign. The higher the difference between your revenue and cost, the more profit you're making. There is one thing to consider though. Google AdWords Conversion Tracking only calculates online conversions via Google and does not include offline transactions or transactions from other networks. If operating a local retail store, there really is no way to track how many people saw your ad and came into your store. The only way to effectively measure in those situations (which I have used a number of times) is to offer a special coupon or 800-number on your ad or landing page.

The next step is to adjust your bids based on the ROI you've calculated. Here is a rule of thumb that may help you get the most from your data:

1. For keywords with ROI under 100 percent: Lowering the cost of your bid may go a long way in improving your ROI. If you think your bid is too high, lower your bid by 20 percent to see if paying less per click will improve profitability.

2. For keywords with ROI over 100 percent: Try increasing bids to see if a higher ad rank will

increase profits. Even though we talked about keeping ads in positions 3–8, you should always experiment with your winning keywords and ads to see if higher ranking will produce more profit.

Chapter Summary

- Tracking your ROI can help you determine which keywords give you the most profit and how to improve your campaign's performance.

- The first step to calculating ROI is to identify and measure your conversions.

- After identifying conversions you can calculate your ROI with one of the formulas provided.

- To accurately determine ROI, you must first determine how to accurately track your conversions and use your ROI data to properly manage your AdWords account.

- Setting up and installing Google Conversion Tracking is easy. All you need to do is place a few lines of code on your Web pages.

- Remember that Google AdWords Conversion Tracking only calculates online conversions via Google and does not include offline transactions.
- Adjust your bids based on the ROI you've calculated.

- If you think your bid is too high, lower your bid by 20 percent

- For keywords with ROI over 100 percent: Try increasing bids to see if a higher ad rank will increase profits.

XII. Scaling Your PPC Program

Once you've created your first profitable PPC campaign, you're well on your way to long-term success. To grow your profits and continue putting more money in your pocket, you need to scale your campaigns. I've used a variety of techniques to scale my winners while at the same time shutting down campaigns that are losing money. Don't discount campaigns too quickly though. I generally don't make any decisions on a campaign unless it's generated something north of 150 clicks.

Here are a few methods that I use to turn up the juice on profitable campaigns. Once you've created a profitable campaign, consider adding one or all of these methods to increase revenue and improve profitability:

1. Increase your daily budgets.
Look at your settings and see if you have any PROFITABLE campaigns that have hit your daily maximum budget, or have even come close within the past thirty days. If you do, raise your daily maximum budget in the campaign. If not, raise the maximum daily spend on the profitable ones anyway, because what you do below may increase spend needed for that campaign anyway.

2. Optimize your campaign settings.
Switch profitable campaign settings to "accelerated" instead of standard—located in the Campaign set up tab. Then, if your profitability holds steady for a few days, you can then safely transition all profitable campaigns to this display method—by priority, the most profitable ones

first—in the Search Partners Network.

3. Expand to other search engines.
Take your profitable campaign and roll it out across other search engines such as Yahoo or Bing. You can even look at search engines such as business.com, superpages.com or consider giving facebook.com a try. The possibilities are endless. Don't attempt to do this until you have a profitable campaign running on Google. Just because you run a campaign on a different network, don't expect it to magically turn from unprofitable to profitable.

4. Add additional keywords.
Use the Google "Quick Add" feature to add new keywords to each ad group or go back to your original keyword analysis to expand your list. Just make sure that after you add these new keywords you use the Duplicate Keyword tool in Google AdWords Editor to get rid of duplicate keywords in your account. Having duplicate keywords in the same account targeting the same geo-targets can hurt your overall campaign performance.

5. Identify any business offerings that are not being promoted.
Look at what your company sells. Are you missing anything? If so, build out campaigns, ad groups, ad copy, keywords, and landing pages around opportunities that you have not promoted in the past.

6. Expand to another geo-target.

Do you serve other areas of the country and the world that you do not currently promote? Expand the geo-targeting options to include new areas. This can be done by setting up new campaigns or by just expanding your settings in an existing one.

7. Expand into the content network.

Be very targeted in how you expand into the content network. Oftentimes, it can bite you. However, if you cast out a net and then quickly clean out the junk by running site placement reports while excluding poor performing sites, you can build a successful campaign over time.

8. Split test landing pages.

You can increase the effectiveness of any profitable campaign by thoroughly testing your landing pages. Google offers yet another free tool to help you improve your conversions called Google Website Optimizer. This tool allows you to test the effectiveness of your landing pages on autopilot.

By applying the techniques described above, you can scale your most profitable campaigns and create additional revenue. When scaling, always start small and watch your data closely to determine which techniques are providing the greatest return on your investment. Different scaling techniques may work for differently based on the product or service being promoted, so always test methods independently.

Chapter Summary

- To grow your profits and put more money in your pocket, you need to scale your campaigns.

- Increase your daily budget on profitable campaigns.

- Optimize campaigns by switching campaign settings to "accelerated" instead of standard.

- Take your profitable campaigns and roll them out across other search engines such as Yahoo or Bing.

- Use the Google "Quick Add" feature to add new keywords to each ad group or go back to your original keyword analysis to expand your list.

- Identify any business offerings (products or services) that are not currently being promoted and consider adding them to a campaign.

- Expand geo-targeting options to include new areas.

- Expand into the Google Content Network.

- Split test landing pages and focus on improving conversions.

XIII. Resources

MyPPCmadesimple.com. Information on pay-per-click marketing and access to bonus videos for individuals who have purchased this book.

Internet Marketing Forum. A great place to find others learning about PPC. Join the forum for free and get help, or give help, with PPC advertising.
http://www.marketingscoop.com/internetmarketingforum

AdWords Help Center: Find answers to commonly asked questions, product guides, and helpful resources at
http://adwords.google.com/support

AdWords Learning Center: View text and multimedia lessons covering all things AdWords at
www.google.com/adwords/learningcenter

Inside AdWords Blog: Stay up to date on the latest AdWords features and developments at
Adwords.blogspot.com

Google Business Channel: Watch educational videos and webinars on AdWords and other Google business solutions at www.youtube.com/googlebusiness

AdWords Success Stories: Find out how other advertisers have used AdWords to grow their businesses through these videos and stories at
www.Adwords.google.com/select/success.html

www.ingramcontent.com/pod-product-compliance
Lightning Source LLC
Chambersburg PA
CBHW052146070326
40689CB00050B/2340